Skillful Means: Wake Up!

Skillful Means: Wake Up!

MASTERING
SUCCESSFUL WORK

Tarthang Tulku

Dharma Publishing

SKILLFUL MEANS SERIES

Skillful Means
Skillful Means: Wake Up!

Library of Congress Cataloging Data

Tarthang Tulku.
   Mastering successful work / Tarthang Tulku.
      Berkeley, CA. : Dharma, c1994.
   xviii, 269 p. ; 22 cm.
   Series title: Skillful means series.
   Work — Psychological aspects.
   Self-actualization (Psychology)

ISBN 0-89800-262-1 (pbk.) ISBN 0-89800-263-X

Typeset in Adobe New Aster and Helvetica Light.
Printed and bound by Dharma Press, Oakland, CA.

9 8 7 6 5 4 3

Contents

Contents

List of Exercises

List of Exercises

List of Exercises

List of Exercises

Preface

Since I came to this country twenty-five years ago, work has been perhaps my greatest teacher. My work has been an inspiration and a challenge, making the journey of my life an education full of rich experience. It would give me great pleasure to be able to share what I have learned in this way with others.

Although I came to the West with a rigorous education in philosophy and religion, I quickly found that to accomplish my goals I would have to master skills in a wide range of practical fields for which I had no training. For those individuals who have chosen to work with me, the same has been true. Time and again we have had to take on a wide range of jobs with no real preparation and few resources. We have found repeatedly that we could be successful despite these obstacles.

Gradually I have realized that our success in this way of working is closely connected to the teachings and the training I received as a young man. Accomplishment in the working world depends on many of the same factors that I had learned to value in my early studies: awareness, concentration, discipline, clarity, and responsibility. All of these are qualities that pay large dividends in both the spiritual and the practical realms.

For our community, developing successful attitudes and approaches in work has served a twofold purpose. First, we are a small group of individuals with very ambitious goals. Only by learning to maximize our efforts and cultivate our skills and resources to the fullest could we hope to accomplish even a small part of what needed to be done. Second, this practice of learning to work effectively has helped to bring the study of the mind alive for my students. In fact, work as a spiritual discipline has become central to what we do.

Someone who sits and meditates may be able to fool himself into thinking he has accomplished more than he has, but someone with a deadline or a payroll to meet cannot get away with bluffing or self-deception. For both my students and myself, work has become a precious opportunity to cultivate our own resources and develop insight and appreciation. Work as a discipline demonstrates perfectly the ancient insight that we must learn to be honest with ourselves if we wish to transform who we are.

Success in work has proved to be a self-sustaining practice. The more we put insights regarding human nature and mental patterns into practice, the more successful we have been in our work; the more our training helped us succeed in the working world, the more we have come to appreciate its value. In this way, we have been able to combine the study of human nature with practical efforts to accomplish our goals. Borrowing a traditional term, I have called this twofold practice 'skillful means'.

In its original meaning, the term 'skillful means' refers to the methods used to bring benefit to all beings, no matter what their circumstances. Skillful means as we practice it has this same quality, for the ways of working we have learned can be of value to everyone. I have seen this again and again in my work with each of our organizations. Communicating and coordinating the details that assure success, interacting with people from all walks of life, I have been able to recognize patterns and implement techniques that seem to apply in every discipline and every kind of work.

Fifteen years ago, I presented some of these insights in a book entitled *Skillful Means*. This small volume has continued to attract interest, and today it remains Dharma Publishing's best-selling title. Most people in this society are painfully aware that they are not getting much benefit out of their work, and there is a great hunger to address this situation. To some small extent, *Skillful Means* may have helped to meet this need.

In the years since then, the issue of how to use work has continued to occupy my attention. With each passing year there seems to be more for our small community to do with the limited resources we have at our disposal. At the same time, we have been able to build on our earlier understanding, exploring more subtle aspects of the interplay among work, awareness, accomplishment, and realization. For several years now, I have been thinking about writing another book on the theme of work that could present some of these insights. I am pleased that this intention has finally taken form.

The guidelines and ideas suggested here are not necessarily new. Anyone who has enjoyed success in his or her work will be familiar with some of them, while anyone who has seriously investigated a spiritual path may be acquainted with others. But there is still a need to understand how these two aspects of life—the practical and the spiritual—can be integrated, so that each can serve the purposes of the other. I am convinced that cherishing work can lead to a way of life that has full meaning, and my hope in writing this book is to communicate this conviction to a larger audience.

In order to benefit from the ideas presented here, it is not necessary to be interested in spiritual concerns. The outlook put forward and the specific suggestions made are intended simply to help people to live cheerfully, work with good results, and profit from knowledge in any circumstance. At the same time, a skillful means approach offers people who are already successful the chance to discover in their work a quality that gives a new sense of meaning to what they are doing.

I also have another purpose in writing this book. During the years I have spent in the West, I have been surprised to discover that many people seem willing to accept a way of living that is not deeply satisfying.

Starting in childhood, they grow used to operating at less than peak effectiveness. Without even realizing it, they cut their own energy, dull their intelligence, and undermine their own best impulses.

Seeing this waste is deeply painful. There is so much important and meaningful work to be done in the world, and so much satisfaction to be found in responding fully to the situations we encounter in our lives. Knowing that this is possible, how can anyone not take action? To deny what we see is to become accomplices in this vast coverup, while to refuse responsibility for how others live their lives is to commit ourselves to a coverup of our own. For this reason, I have felt a strong wish to share some of the insights I have been fortunate enough to discover in the years I have lived and worked in this great land.

The specific ideas presented here trace back about twelve years, when I began exploring a systematic approach to awareness, concentration, and energy as factors in accomplishment. In 1985, I put together a set of essays on these topics called *Diamond Keys*, meant particularly for workers at Odiyan, our country center. This summer, having returned from an extended trip abroad, I decided to take up and rework this material. Working with Zara Wallace as the principal editor, I combined these older essays with substantial new material to create the present volume.

The resulting approach cuts across such disciplines as management, psychology, communications studies, and spirituality. I am convinced it can be of use to almost anyone and in virtually every discipline. I have tried to keep the material presented open-ended, for it is my firm conviction that each of us already has the experience or knowledge needed to be successful. Even if we have only had a single experience of real success in our work, we can build on that instance; even if we know more than we care to admit about failure, we can learn from our mistakes. We can all share what we know with one another. Together, we can discover countless treasures—innovative approaches and creative thoughts that can become our friends and counselors.

This book is dedicated to all who work, especially on the spiritual path, and to the members of the Nyingma community, whose tireless work on behalf of the goals we share has been an inspiration to me. Our work together has given me the opportunity to bring these topics together. I hope that these ideas will bear abundant fruit for each of them, furthering their development and endowing them with the capacity for limitless success. May this work bring ease to many people, and may it help them to improve the quality of awareness, concentration, and energy in all aspects of their work and life.

Tarthang Tulku
December 1993

A Note to Readers

This book is meant to be of benefit to several different audiences, and not everyone will want to read it through from cover to cover. Part One introduces the basic themes and should be read by everyone. Part Two contains material that should be useful to most readers, but also includes suggestions for people unfamiliar with business, and can be read selectively by those with business experience. Part Three deepens and extends the major themes of the book, while Part Four includes more advanced supplemental exercises that some readers may not be interested in. The list of Good Business Practices included at the end of the book should be most useful for people just starting out in business or setting up their own organizations or projects.

Exercises and Journal

Practical exercises are an integral part of this book. Most of them are meant to be done more than once, and to be practiced regularly whenever possible. The majority of the exercises appear in the text and are related to the material that they accompany.

A Note to Readers

A set of fundamental exercises called Tools for Change is collected at the end of the book; some of them are introduced at specific points in the text, but they can all be practiced at any time with good results. A second set of exercises, also at the end of the book, is called Tools for Troubled Times; these exercises are especially useful for coping with crises and difficulties. A complete list of exercises appears after the table of contents.

It is recommended that readers seriously interested in deepening their approach to work through careful study of this book keep a journal. Making regular journal entries is a way to record your discoveries and see your progress in the adventure of training the mind and bringing awareness to work. When you can see where you have been and what you have learned, you can move with confidence into the future. Keeping a journal also expresses your willingness to take responsibility for your own training, evaluate your progress, and consciously make improvements in the light of new insight.

Further Training

For information on training programs that deepen the approaches introduced in this book and information regarding on-site training, write to the Nyingma Institute, 1815 Highland Place, Berkeley CA 94709.

Skillful Means: Wake Up!

A New Way
of Working

Most people work primarily for the income they earn. Of course, work fulfills additional needs as well: the status of a professional identity, the approval of others, a sense of power and mastery, social interaction, and the simple satisfaction of keeping busy. What all these rewards share is that they are extrinsic to the process of working itself. We work to accomplish particular goals, but we seldom find value in the actual activity of working.

This way of working is impoverishing at a deep level. When work as an activity is not valued for its own sake, we rarely work with real enjoyment or a sense of rich fulfillment. Satisfying moments do come, but they soon pass, leaving only the memory of well-being.

Perhaps this is why people who have worked hard and successfully for many years sometimes come to a point where they question the value of what they have been doing. Their effort has given them a degree of material security and comforts, but has it helped them to develop as human beings? Has it deepened their sense of meaning and purpose? Has it allowed them to get any closer to fulfilling their goals in life? These are not easy questions to have to face.

When we work without real willingness, work is ultimately not very rewarding. We have to force ourselves to do what we do, and this internal conflict leads to exhaustion in spirit and mind that numbs our senses and deprives us of pleasure in the rest of our lives as well. Working with resistance, we are naturally inefficient, and our work tends to head in the direction of mediocrity and failure rather than excellence and success.

Even if we work for a cause that we believe in, this same pattern persists. Although we may work with much more energy and commitment, we look past the actual activity of working to its results. Seldom do we consider that work itself could be a chance to learn something fundamental about ourselves or give us the opportunity to demonstrate compassion or be an example for others.

Most of us take for granted that we are working for our own benefit, but in fact we do not seem very skillful at satisfying our own needs and wants. We have settled for a lifestyle in which most of our time is dedicated to an activity that we find only partially rewarding. We look for real satisfaction outside of work, putting our lives on hold during the time we are doing our job. Seeking happiness in the margins of our lives, we wind up supporting such negative patterns as addiction and escapism. Work may give us temporary forms of ego gratification, but there is another, deeper part of ourselves that we are failing to nourish. No wonder so many people sense that something is out of balance in their lives.

The culture that I come from offered a clear alternative to these ways of working. Although ordinary occupations were respected, those who sought a more meaningful way of life could choose to withdraw from worldly concerns completely, pursuing a way of life devoted to religious practice and inquiry. Such individuals often seemed to find a special joy and inspiration in what they did: an inner sense of spiritual peace and well-being more meaningful than success in the practical realm.

In this society, alternatives to the world of work are also available. Even if few people today withdraw from the world completely, there are always some who devote themselves to a more spiritual path, whether it is linked to religion, art, service, or the pursuit of knowledge. Rejecting material pursuits and the practical world of business, they seek rewards that they consider more closely linked to the fundamental significance of human existence.

The separation between these two ways of life has long gone unquestioned, but in today's world, such a division is simply no longer workable. The strict hierarchies and shared beliefs that supported it in the past are vanishing. Spiritual communities and individuals cannot afford to leave worldly affairs to others, for they can no longer count on support from the larger society. Nor do most individuals working in the world draw sustenance from the efforts of those who attend to the concerns of the spirit, for the sense of deep connection between the spiritual and the worldly realms is lacking.

As the trend toward social fragmentation accelerates and spreads to every part of the world, the consequences of this split between spiritual and worldly are severe. On the one hand, spiritual values become increasingly marginalized. It becomes ever more difficult for those concerned with spiritual matters and questions of ultimate concern to find the material support that will let them pursue this path. On the other hand, the tremendous accomplishments of this culture in the material realm come to seem hollow, undermined by a growing sense of meaninglessness and dissatisfaction and a suspicion that the social fabric is close to unravelling.

Based on the experience that I have had since coming to the West twenty-five years ago, I am convinced that this split between the world of work and the concerns of the spirit is not necessary. Work itself can have inner meaning and value that make it part of the spiritual path. Anyone who does any kind of work can taste the sense of deep inner fulfillment that has always been considered the fruit of a spiritual way of living, even if he or she feels no sense of religious vocation. There is no need to put up with the pain and emptiness that so many people experience today, and there is a far more meaningful alternative to our increasingly desperate attempts to fill the hole within our hearts.

What is more, learning to integrate spiritual values into work can be a powerful way to assure that our work will be successful on its own terms. The more fully work expresses the beauty of an inner ethic, the more effective and productive it can be.

This prospect of benefit at every level is the vision that guides this book. Work does not have to be a painful necessity or a dirty word. If we use work to challenge our limits, to perfect awareness and deepen concentration, then work can open into knowledge that makes us more successful while also nourishing us at the deepest levels. By letting work guide us toward deeper knowledge, we can end each day with a sense of enjoyment and a feeling that we have accomplished something of real benefit. We can achieve our own goals and set an example that has the potential to transform society.

The Inner Practice of Work

The organic link between work and spiritual values becomes more clear as soon as we ask what it is that people really want out of life. At this fundamental level, there is really little difference between the business world and the spiritual realm. People want to be happy, to accomplish something of value in their lives, and to live in a way that is healthy and balanced. Though the language used to describe business and spiritual goals and the vision of how to achieve these goals may be very different, this fundamental connection is there.

The means for attaining these goals are also closely related. Happiness and the ability to achieve something of value both depend on the capacities of the mind. Without knowing how to educate, nourish, and discipline these inborn capacities, we can accomplish little in either the spiritual realm or the business world.

For example, the power of prayer depends on an ability to focus the mind. To develop this ability, we must learn contemplation, going deeply into a feeling or an image or concern without relying on words and reasons. This same skill under a different name is equally vital to business success.

Once we recognize these similarities, we see that nothing prevents work from being a path to knowledge. The study of mind has traditionally been the province of a small minority in society, but in today's democratic times we can see it quite differently. We are all human beings aiming at similar goals; by the same token, we can all direct our efforts toward attaining knowledge, each in our own ways.

Over the past two decades, working with my students in a wide variety of projects and businesses, I have found this link between spiritual values and work to hold in every area. Based on our experience, I can say with confidence that when we join work and spiritual practice, there is progress in both directions. This is no marriage of convenience, but a union that can help us fulfill our life's destiny. Success in one area goes together with success in the other, for the knowledge essential to both is one and the same. Walking both paths at once, we can let that knowledge flower and gather its rich nectar.

This seems to me to be a major discovery, or perhaps a rediscovery of knowledge that has been lost in our time. True, a long tradition of Western thought holds that daily work can be charged with spiritual significance. Yet this way of understanding sanctifies work in terms of its role in a divine order, rather than as a spiritual path in its own right. In any event, there are many people today for whom this form of religious belief no longer carries conviction.

The approach suggested here is quite different. Work can be united with our ultimate concerns more directly, as a path of exploration and discovery similar to the path of prayer or the path of meditation that might have been followed in other times and places. Working in this way, we can develop the tools for success in whatever we do.

When we rely on work as our practice, we get direct, immediate feedback that is remarkably useful on any kind of spiritual path. The 'bottom line' mentality of business, with its focus on action and results, makes it very difficult for us to fool ourselves. What is more, the steady challenges of work force us to develop more knowledge. For example, the need to be effective in dealing with others means that we have to become students of mind. The need to improve on our mistakes means that we have to be honest about our own strengths and weaknesses.

Choosing not to use our work as a training ground in this way is not a real option. When people fail to learn from the lessons that work teaches, they sow the seeds for failure and dissatisfaction on the practical level, and lose the opportunity to find real meaning and deep fulfillment on the spiritual level. Perhaps many of us do live in just this way, but there is no reason that this has to continue.

When work becomes a path to realization and fulfillment, our actions become meaningful from moment to moment. We cut through the paralyzing sense that time spent working is time taken away from our real concerns and interests, and win back control over half our lives. Now we can really look out for ourselves. Instead of setting ourselves up for disappointment and frustration, we can serve our own best interests in all that we do.

At the same time, we lay the groundwork for a natural transformation in the nature of work. Without giving up the focus on success, we learn to work in ways that are more humane, more fulfilling, and more cooperative. We learn to act in harmony with our own deep concerns, to respect the environment that shelters and provides for us, and to care for the needs of others.

The lessons we learn from work often have to do with our mistakes and failures, but these can be the most important lessons of all. Perhaps what we see are the ways that we cheat ourselves in working: the excuses and the laziness, the tension and worry, the backing down and putting off. If so, we can profit tremendously from our experience. Aware of what we are doing, we can form the intention to change and develop the discipline to do so. At that point, work becomes our lifeline to transformation—the means through which we can improve our way of thinking, our attitudes, our relationships, and our actions.

Through work we can test immediately whether the changes we make are effective. We can see what works and what does not, and we can put into practice whatever produces the best result. At the same time, we learn the power of a positive attitude and outlook. How could we ask for a better schooling?

Work has value for every aspect of human being. Through our work, we can invite a rich and healthy way of living, founded in the abundance of awareness, concentration, and energy. The wealth that comes through this way of being banishes for all time the sense that our lives are impoverished. Whatever our external circumstances, we are ready to go forward, moving steadily toward fulfillment.

The path of inquiry that work opens is available even if our daily responsibilities seem to offer no outlet for our natural creativity. Perhaps our present job is not suited to us; perhaps we have no job. Still, we can learn from what we do not have as well as what we have. We do not need to look for some special set of circumstances or for the perfect job; we can start right now.

For example, we are all familiar with the fears and tensions, the anxieties and self-doubts that eat away at our well-being and undermine our ability to be productive. Right now we can take steps to cut through those hopeless and helpless ways of being. Like an athlete training for competition, we can train ourselves in awareness, concentration, and energy, so that we will be prepared when circumstances allow us to manifest the power of our intrinsic creativity and knowledge.

Perhaps these sound like lofty goals. But we do have the resources we need, and they are available right now. Perhaps this book can help you see this. If you bring into your life the ideas, practices, and ways of working presented here, tension, worry, and other barriers to achievement may loosen their grip on your consciousness. If you chew and digest well the suggestions made here, contemplating their meanings, visualizing the different steps of each process, and applying the resulting insights in your work, then your daily life will become knowledge, the activity of skillful means.

The final responsibility is yours. If you think that change will come by doing what someone else has told you to do; if you try to follow a plan that an author imposes on you, you will never fulfill your own destiny. Instead, stay with your own understanding. By cultivating awareness and concentration and energy, you will touch the integrity of your own being and take control of your own life.

I am convinced that what is written here can help you. But in the end it is up to you to write your own book, drawing on your intentions, your commitment, and your growing understanding. As you activate knowledge, you can shape these elements through action and accomplishment. You can embark on a heroic journey of vast dimensions.

PART ONE

Waking Up
to Knowledge

The Gift
of Knowledge

Each of us alive today has been given the special opportunity of birth in a time of great transitions. The cultures of this planet are drawing closer together, and rich treasures of knowledge are entering our world from all directions, passed on to us by every civilization and every generation throughout human history.

We have the potential to benefit from the best of this knowledge and to preserve it for the future. Within our minds and bodies we carry the fullness of human intelligence, with its open-ended potential for understanding. We have the capacity to activate knowledge, embody it in our lives, and transmit it for the benefit of others.

The vehicle we need to do this is already available to us. The work that we do to provide for our own livelihood and to develop our skills can be the skillful means for bringing knowledge into the world.

Each of us has the ability to design and embody dynamic patterns of work that express our intelligence in action. By cultivating our inner resources as we work, we can enjoy success in what we do, increase satisfaction in our lives, and generate a lighter and healthier way of being. Drawing on the full range of knowledge that is our human inheritance, we can make a lasting contribution to our society and our world.

When the depth of our intelligence and caring shines through our work, life becomes enriched and balanced. Guided by inner knowledge and illumined by insight, our attitudes and actions move naturally toward fulfillment. Rather than relying on opinions and beliefs or looking outside ourselves for direction, we can base our lives on this trustworthy source of insight and understanding. We can embody the values that give life wholeness and meaning.

The Roots of Knowledge

Work teaches us to cultivate the roots of our knowledge in an organic way that fosters the continuing growth of understanding and brings it to maturity. When we know how to use work in this way, we can nourish and enjoy ourselves in any situation, like a great chef creating delicious meals from all kinds of foods.

We can also learn from the past in a new way, not only studying history in order to learn lessons that can be applied in the future, but also bringing knowledge gained from past mistakes alive in the present moment. Human beings have not always been successful in learning from the past, and the advantages of discovering how to maximize this neglected resource would be enormous, for society as well as ourselves. Instead of repeating past mistakes, we could benefit from lost opportunities, stop unproductive behaviors, and create better ways of living and working in the present and future.

To make work creative and satisfying in these ways, we must be willing to take responsibility for how we are using work in our lives. Each of us needs to think through for ourselves why we work and whether we truly wish to bring our full energy and resolve to our work. If we take seriously the opportunity it offers, work can become a pathway to knowledge rich in satisfaction and accomplishment. If at the same time we cultivate a global vision, putting knowledge into action with compassion and sincere conviction, we can connect our work to the highest spiritual goals.

Restoring the Dynamic of Knowledge

The knowledge active in our times seems to be moving us toward a society that will be colder and more limited in mind and spirit than our own, one where the limitless possibilities of knowledge could be closed off and even forgotten. While the trend toward technological achievements has led to a vast expansion of one specific kind of knowledge, it is also promoting the rapid disappearance of differences among cultures. From this perspective, the range of human knowledge appears to be shrinking. What is more, technological knowledge creates unpredictable side-effects that are difficult to control. As the cultures of the world begin to merge into one global culture, and technological knowledge moves to the forefront, these limitations on our knowledge will manifest with increasing momentum, and problems will proliferate exponentially.

The limitations of contemporary knowledge are evident not only in our global situation but also in the quality of our lives. No matter how we spend our time, most of us experience great tension in our bodies and minds. Like warriors of worry, we battle ourselves internally, bruising our minds and senses with anxious thoughts and negative judgments that prevent us from responding fully to experience. Pressured by time each day, we are hardly able to enjoy the little leisure left to us. When problems arise that we are unable to solve, we have few alternatives to discouragement, numbness, cynicism, or despair. This way of life is not very productive nor is it satisfying. Do we really want to abuse our short time on earth in this way?

Given the extent of the difficulties we face today, on both the personal and global levels, it may be tempting to withdraw from active responsibility or to deny that anything significant can change. But these responses, which themselves express the limitations of our knowledge, are profoundly dangerous, for they condemn us to inaction and stagnation. The healthier response is to wake up knowledge in the conduct of our livelihood.

In an era when traditional forms of knowledge are being abandoned, making work into a path of knowledge is the natural way to embody and promote understanding. Each of us can test and refine our experience as we work, looking for reliable sources of knowledge that we can share with one another and pass on to our children. Our work is the laboratory for such experiments, the testing ground for the values we profess and seek to put into practice. If we choose a way of working that is also a way of learning and inquiring, enjoying and accomplishing, we are making a commitment to knowledge that can ultimately have global benefits.

In the decades ahead, as technology becomes increasingly sophisticated, the gap between those whose work is by nature creative and challenging and those who are cut off from meaning in what they do seems certain to widen. If we can demonstrate through our own example that work can be a path of knowledge, we can help restore meaning to all kinds of work. We can show that work does not have to be routine and meaningless for anyone. As the vehicle through which each individual participates in the growth of knowledge, work can be a way for each of us to manifest our own vision of what has meaning and make a unique contribution to society.

Using work in this way supports a cooperative approach to the development of knowledge. In today's workplace, the motivation for discovering new knowledge is primarily competitive. But this motivation is inherently limited, and the knowledge it gives access to operates within a narrow range. In the global community that is coming into being, cooperation for the benefit of all peoples is far more likely to have long-lasting positive results. By infusing our life's work with a spirit of cooperation, we can pledge our support to the knowledge that will support all the world's peoples.

Cooperation comes naturally when we are committed to developing our knowledge through work, for then friendly accommodation becomes the norm, even within the framework of competition. If we turn instead toward maintaining our own positions, strengthening competition rather than cooperation, we may lose the opportunity to activate new patterns of understanding in our lives.

In this changing world, knowledge is our only reliable refuge and the only real source of success. It is the key to activating our inner resources, so that we can live in a more sane and balanced way. Having inherited the knowledge of the past, we have a responsibility to use that knowledge to enrich our lives and transmit what we learn to others. If we shape our work with intelligence and act with integrity and strength, we can work in ways that improve the quality of knowledge itself. As time propels us into the future, we can ensure that the benefits of knowledge will be available to all.

Waking Up to Time

Every minute and every hour, time is passing. Once time has occupied a particular moment, that moment is gone forever. In the back of our minds, we think that time is always available, and we imagine that lost time can somehow be replaced—that we can 'make up for it' tomorrow or next week. But we cannot borrow time from the future. Once time is gone, we can never get it back.

Although we have units to measure time, we cannot readily take hold of its dynamic energy. This is because we are not ready to acknowledge that time is passing right now, and that our lives are passing along with it. We often go about our business as if we had a few extra minutes in our back pocket to pull out when we really need them. But an hour is sixty minutes and no more; a day is twenty-four hours, not twenty-five; a year is twelve months, not thirteen. Our time is limited, and each moment is irreplaceable. When we let ourselves see this, we have started on the path of knowledge that leads to success and transformation.

When we think as businesspeople and professionals, we know that each moment has value: that 'time is money'. But our ordinary consciousness does not feed back to us the deeper knowledge that time is our life—our blood, our heart, our senses. If we want to accomplish something of value with our lives, opening our awareness to time at this deeper level is the place to start. When we feel the urgency of acting right now, we will make the best use of the time available to us.

Learning to incorporate time into our consciousness and to bring this awareness into our work is a vital task in today's world, when shortages of time are commonplace and the pressure of time's relentless momentum bears down on us all. By learning to connect to time's flow and act in accord with it, we can transform this pressure. We can come into harmony with the boundless energy of time and use it for our own best purposes.

Time Past and Time Future

How have we used our time so far: What have we really accomplished in our lives? If we try to reconstruct the last few years, what achievements stand out? Looking back, we see that our memories are mostly vague and indistinct. Whole weeks and months seem to have passed by like a dream. Even entire decades leave only a few main impressions. While we were living out those days and hours, we may have focused our efforts on collecting and enjoying certain kinds of experiences or possessions, but now that the time is gone, what do we have to show for it? Reflecting on how easily time can disappear without leaving behind any lasting accomplishment, we may find ourselves asking: Is this how I want to live for the rest of my life?

In each moment we have the opportunity to act on our highest values. Within our present situation and our current responsibilities, we can turn our energy toward goals that really matter to us; we can develop our awareness and cultivate knowledge that benefits everyone. We know from personal experience that using time in meaningful ways is deeply enjoyable; we know that productive work freely carried out satisfies and fulfills our heart and spirit. Acting on this knowledge, we can commit ourselves to making the best possible use of our time. Unless we make that commitment, it is difficult to see how we will ever be able to accomplish much of value.

How Much Time Do We Have Left?

It may seem that we still have decades available to accomplish our goals, but this way of looking is deceptive. If we calculate day by day, how much time is actually available for fruitful activity?

To start with, there is the time spent eating, sleeping, and doing routine tasks, as well as the time lost to disruptions such as illness. Out of a twenty-four-hour day, these activities probably eat up at least half of our time, leaving us a total of twelve hours that we could think of as our productive day. What really happens during these twelve hours?

First come the little things that nibble away at the day: commuting, making small repairs and running errands, waiting in line, doing busywork, redoing work that was not done right to begin with, and completing work that was not finished on time. Then there are the recreations and entertainments, which may be pleasant at the time, but disappear without a trace. Once we subtract these activities, we may have about eight hours left for work that gives us a real return on our investment of energy.

But if five minutes of each remaining hour are spent in confusion or hesitation, we lose almost an hour. If another five minutes or so are spent in idle talking, we lose another hour. Ten minutes more invested in daydreams, grudges, or worries takes another chunk out of the time available. Now we have about five or six hours to accomplish something worthwhile. Can we get back in six hours enough satisfying accomplishment for the whole day?

Even this time is not fully available. Emotionality runs through our day as grain runs through wood, creating pockets of resistance and unhappiness that undermine our effectiveness. Moments of joy, delight, and inspiration alternate with negative thoughts and feelings. There are times when our concentration settles and feelings of confidence and stability begin to form, but at other times we are too caught up in reactions and judgments to focus on what needs to be done.

Most of us are not used to focusing on this inner level of activity. If we look as though we are working, if our body is going through the right motions and our mind is roughly directed toward the right concerns, we consider that we have spent our time well. But what of the negative thoughts and feelings that limit our productivity and steal away our pleasure? What of the steady stream of internal distractions? Should we really accept as a given that our awareness is dim, our concentration interrupted, and our energy diverted?

Try tracing out for yourself what your mind does with an hour of time, checking back every five minutes or so. You may be deeply surprised, even shocked, to see how many minutes slip away as you tell stories, register complaints, play out fantasies and inner dialogues, watch internal images, and react to the dramatic overtones that emotions impose on each new experience. When we factor in this level of activity, we realize that we may have only three hours left out of the six that we thought were available. In fact, even this estimate may be too generous.

At this point we have only about a quarter of the productive day left to us. Consider what this means. If we were measuring physical abilities instead of time, operating at one-fourth of our capacity would be considered a severe handicap. If we could really work at full capacity instead, we have been doing ourselves a grave disservice. Every task takes four times too long to complete. Four people are required to do what one fully functioning person could accomplish alone.

We could also look at it this way: If we have forty years of productive activity left, this is really only the equivalent of ten years of full accomplishment. If we have ten years, we are actually down to less than three years. Can we count on achieving the goals we have set for ourselves in this span of time? If we really care about what we are doing, how can we accept operating at this level of inefficiency?

Finally, we need to consider that if we could work with more consistency and fewer disruptions, our concentration would deepen and our awareness expand, and we could give more steady energy to whatever we are doing. Working in this way, we might be able to double our productive capacities. This means that we actually have the potential to do eight times as much as we are doing right now!

Perhaps it sounds as though we are writing a prescription for burn-out and drudgery: all work and no play. But if we reflect on our past experience, we realize that the times when we work at peak efficiency and with full concentration are also times when we feel joyful and fulfilled. The more we do, the more we want to do, and the more energy and resources for accomplishment we discover.

Why are we missing out on the opportunity to live and act in these ways? For a preliminary answer, we can look to our deliberate choice to ignore the role time plays in our lives.

Even though resistance to acknowledging time's passage is rooted deep within our consciousness, we are free to challenge it. We can increase our awareness of time until we can actually sense time passing from moment to moment. With this new awareness of time, new options open before us. Aware that we have no time to waste, we can resolve to focus our efforts and find better ways to use our energy. Instead of making excuses, seeking out distractions, or giving in to negative emotions, we can build up confidence in our own skill and knowledge. Then change will come quickly.

Exercise 1 Daily Schedule

The rhythm of rising, eating, working, and sleeping creates a framework for effective action that connects our lives to time. Within this framework, create a daily schedule that maps out time for work, reflection, family responsibilities, and other activities that are important to you. Once you have made this schedule and experimented with it for a few days, resolve to stay closely within it for at least two weeks. When you break the schedule, take time to reflect carefully on what has happened to bring this about.

After a while, the schedule you have established may become quite routine. At that point, look to see how you can make it more complete or more challenging; ask yourself what level of care you are putting into it.

Exercise 2 Reviewing Accomplishments

Waking up to time depends on giving yourself accurate feedback on how you are using your time. Each evening for two weeks set aside a few minutes to review what you have accomplished during the day. Look for periods when you wasted time, but also for occasions when you had a sense of working or acting with full energy, in harmony with the flow of time. Include in your review feelings of satisfaction, frustration, or disappointment, without making them the focus. Let the resulting awareness of time inspire you to engage more fully in your work.

Exercise 3   Condensing Time

Imagine that an average human lifespan is only one year in length. Cultivate a sense of the richness of a whole lifetime—the growth, the accomplishment, and the understanding—being condensed into twelve short months. Reflect on how precious this brief life is and how urgent it is to make good use of the time you have left.

Now condense that knowing even further, imagining that the week to come will be a lifetime. Bring this sense of condensed time into the actual rhythms and events of the week. Maintaining this focus can help you develop the awareness you need to wake up to time right now.

Taking Control
of Time

Using time well gives focus and energy to our actions, so that we can apply ourselves to the fullest and get the best return on our investment. Working becomes healthy and productive, and we are successful without having to make special efforts to succeed. This is the practice of skillful means: a way of working that challenges our abilities, overcomes obstacles, transforms resistance and negativities, and offers inspiration to us and to others through creative accomplishment.

By taking time to heart, we learn to connect work to time in a new way. We engage work as an exercise and opportunity, using it to generate innovative knowledge and refine a comprehensive sense of responsibility. We profit from experience, educating ourselves in the understanding and vision that can give us reliable guidance. Working becomes a way of life that steadily opens to new insights.

Sidetracking the Dynamic of Time

Our usual ways of working are ineffective precisely because they are missing this connection with time. Although we may make strong efforts to organize every minute tightly, we tend to impose these efforts from outside, rather than learning to work with the inner dynamic of time. Eventually such structures will break down.

Without having the dynamic of time on our side, we are unable to maintain consistent energy and steady efforts over time, and cannot carry our original intentions through to the best results. We may plan well and begin well but not follow through, so that our work deteriorates. Or we may start off poorly and gradually improve, but lose time and energy in efforts to recover from the mistakes we made at the outset. If we do not finish a job on time, a new priority may force us to put it aside. Left as unfinished business, it is more difficult to take up again; when we do return to it, we cannot remember exactly where we were, our interest and caring have dissipated, or we have forgotten the instructions we received earlier. We have to struggle to generate new momentum, and by the time we finish, we are already behind schedule on the next task.

Another clear indication that we do not have time on our side is that knowledge becomes sidetracked and unavailable. The information we need is lost in piles of memos, hidden on a computer disk, or buried in notebooks no one reads. If laziness, reluctance, or competitiveness prevent us from organizing information well enough for someone else to understand, knowledge never enters the stream of time to begin with. Once we find ourselves running behind time, we may deliberately divert knowledge from the rhythm of time, holding back what we know because we are not confident we can handle the consequences of setting new activity in motion.

Breakdown Dynamic

When awareness is disconnected from time, work meets with obstacles or blockages that we cannot control. If we investigate these difficulties, we find one kind of breakdown after another. Perhaps the equipment malfunctions or someone gets sick; perhaps the instructions we received are not accurate or transportation has not been properly coordinated; perhaps the plan we set in motion does not work or the goal we set is not clear; perhaps we do not understand what needs to be done or responsibility has not been delegated adequately.

On the surface, such problems may not seem connected to time, but in almost every case the difficulty or its impact could have been prevented by timely action. The equipment could have been properly maintained; the person out with illness could have passed on essential information; the instructions or plans could have been tested in advance. Now it is too late.

As work turns into an ongoing series of emergencies, our efforts to achieve our major goals give way to damage control. Time is spent in stop-gap measures: putting out fires, plugging leaks, and filling cracks. There is no possibility for creative action or for enjoying the flow of productivity because all our resources go into catching up, repairing mistakes,

31

and adjusting our plans. The cycle is self-perpetuating: We do not have time to make a good plan because our time is taken up dealing with the flaws in the old plan; we cannot clear up our communication because we are processing the emotions stirred up by previous communications.

Once we fall behind time, energetic momentum cannot build. As we rush from one thing to another, our concentration is weak and our awareness shallow. Since our productivity remains low, we feel dissatisfied, resentful, or worthless. We become increasingly moody and emotional, ready to blame ourselves or others for being ineffective. If the situation is bad enough, we feel unable to think clearly, focus, or act. Our bodies rebel: The head and neck ache, the shoulders are tight, the back is in spasm, the stomach is upset. In our endless internal dialogues, we repeat fragments of emotionally charged messages over and over again: "I'm sick and tired of this," "I don't know what to do," "It's all their fault," "How could they do that to me?"

Working in this way has nothing to offer but frustration. We operate on a surface level, unable to penetrate to the creative heart of our work. We cannot stand to see our lack of progress, so we stop looking and stop caring, and fall out of touch with time completely. We inhabit a dull, deadened space. We are almost certain to miss the target, because we are not even trying to hit it. Knowledge, intelligence, confidence, joy, and encouragement are someone else's department.

Renewing the Dynamic of Time

The antidote to these negative patterns is to bring knowledge directly into the flow of time. This means starting with knowledge of time itself: not as an abstraction, but as the dynamic flow of work and action that we encounter every day. By being precise and clear about the relation of work to time, and by challenging the ways we usually relate to time, we can train awareness in the sharpness and speed that let us master time's momentum.

We cannot touch the dynamism of time when we feel casual about our work or have a vague, unstructured plan for our day. If that is how we work, our looseness invites interruptions and obstacles, almost welcoming them as good excuses. Instead, we need to be focused on our aim, so that awareness can connect directly to time and our energy can awaken to its dynamic.

We all have experience with this way of working. When we are intent on meeting a deadline, racing against the clock, we experience time with direct urgency. The following exercise uses this 'deadline energy' as a 'lifeline' to the dynamic of time.

Exercise 4   Lifeline of Time

At the beginning of the day, set a series of dead-lines. For instance, you might set a firm goal for each hour. Focus on the goal and invite the urgent energy of the deadline into awareness. In this way, you can use the power of every moment. If you set a series of deadlines throughout the day, you can regenerate this dynamic all day long. Promise yourself to meet each goal, so that you reactivate the feeling of urgency again and again. You may expect to fail, but awareness and concentration will come to the rescue, naturally strengthening and sharpening your effort and intention. If you miss a deadline, set it again or go on to the next. Do not cut the momentum.

This exercise gives practice in setting realistic targets and meeting them, an essential tool for developing awareness and increasing levels of concentration and energy. Once you gain confidence in this way of working, review your schedule for the week and make it more precise, setting deadlines in the same way. You could also do the same for your monthly schedule.

Often when people do this exercise, they benefit tremendously from the surge of energy that comes from setting a goal and meeting it. Not only are they much more productive, but they also feel a great sense of well-being and harmony. Yet despite this experience, most people initially have difficulty in continuing with the exercise for more than a day or two. If this is your experience, ask yourself what is going on. Why would you turn away from a practice that has such a positive impact?

One reason people give for holding back from complete involvement with time is that they think working at top speed will lower the quality of their results. Most likely, however, this view is based on recalling the 'skidding' sensation of working at high speed with poor concentration and unclear awareness. When you work dynamically, combining speed with a light focus that helps to deepen concentration and sustain energy, the quality of your work will improve, not deteriorate. You will also find that making maximum efforts actually increases your energy.

Just as gold ore must be refined to become pure gold, the awareness, concentration, and energy that assure us of success require heating and cooling, stretching and hammering, shaping and polishing to bring out their finest qualities. The dynamic of time applies these purifying energies. Like the tremendous pressures that transform carbon into diamonds, deadlines can train us to be masters rather than victims of time.

Inviting Time

If we were yogis living outside human society, we might structure our relationship to time without regard to schedules. But that is a different story told in a different realm. In these demanding times, our challenge is to awaken the knowledge that will let us draw on time's dynamic. Then we can use our energy skillfully, exercise our abilities joyfully, and truly cherish our accomplishments.

Once we are able to use time effectively, we do not need to structure time with the same intensity. Freely inviting time to enter our being, we can relax deeply within the pressure of our work, opening space for time's energy. Awareness can dance with time loosely and lightly, moment by moment, growing ever brighter and clearer. No tightness, fears, or worries interrupt the dynamic flow of energy.

Relaxing into time lets us enjoy ourselves so fully that we get results without special effort. Like a professional dancer who loves dancing, we enjoy challenging ourselves while working. We appreciate the flavor of each movement and gesture, each routine and each requirement. Work becomes a partnership in which body and senses, intelligence and awareness all participate in a light and harmonious way. Savoring this lightness and balance, we build strength and confidence and learn to encourage ourselves in whatever we do.

Exercise 5 Developing Stability

Often the pressure of time makes us feel so tense and tight that we have no room to consider other ways to be. The following exercise can help counteract this response. You can do it any time you find a few quiet minutes at work.

Sitting quietly, relax the mind and body, and gradually develop the feeling that the organs of the body are floating—suspended in the ocean or in space. Let awareness contact this silent spaciousness. Feel it in your body and let it deepen into a sense of rich stability. Let tension dissolve into these rich feelings. If you want to take this feeling further, you can imagine that the inside of your body merges with space, or that it is filled with light.

Exercise 6   Charting Time

A. For one month keep track of the work you do hour by hour. Each hour, stop and make a brief note in a daily log. Be rigorously honest about what you have really accomplished. Review the results to see how you use time and how you are sidetracked from your goals. Learn to be deeply familiar with the way time manifests in your work.

B. During the following month, continue to chart work hour by hour as before, but also make a brief hourly plan at the start of each day for what you intend to do that day. At the end of the day, compare the plan and the reality. Computer software is available that can help simplify this task.

Exercise 7   Setting Targets

When you have several jobs to do in one day, or even in a single hour, take each task, set a reasonable time limit for it, and then try to do it within the specified time. If you do not succeed, you may need to develop better awareness and energy. Are you setting reasonable targets? Are you using maximum energy to accomplish each task? When does resistance come up? At what points do you feel tired? What happens then?

Exercise 8   Just Do It

Sometimes a careful plan is required to accomplish a job, but at other times you can just do it immediately without any wasted thought or talk.

There is a rule in office management that you should never handle a piece of paper more than once: See if you can meet that standard. The more you stay swiftly and neatly on top of things, the sooner you will see results. For the next month, see how many jobs you can handle as they come up, in just a few minutes. Be careful to stay balanced so that you do not let such tasks distract you from the main focus of what you are doing. Keep track of how you do.

For more exercises on using time, see Tools for Change, pp. 251–52.

Developing Awareness

Once we have made the commitment to bring awareness to time, there are many techniques and approaches we can use. Before we can apply them with real effectiveness, however, we must learn to focus our awareness more fully. Otherwise our efforts will be sporadic and the results unpredictable. One day we may set deadlines and successfully meet them, but the next day we may forget to set deadlines altogether. Our awareness is simply not strong enough to sustain our efforts.

Focused awareness is the master key to every higher level of achievement. It gives us the power to sort through experience and act on what has value, and it allows us to create the discipline and structure that support accomplishment.

Waking Up from the Dream

Life has a predictable, routine quality that is very dreamlike. We seem to have settled on ways of living and acting that depend on dullness, on not being clear about what is happening in our lives. As one day merges into the next, the details of experience are lost, and the results of our actions prove hard to measure. Habitual patterns drain our actions of power and effectiveness. Living in this way, we cannot generate the knowledge that could wake us up to a sense of higher purpose and possibility.

When we acknowledge the dynamic of time and resolve to use it more effectively, we are taking a first step toward countering this dreamy dullness. We are making a commitment to awareness and to applying its power in this very moment.

Humanity has a special affinity for awareness and the knowledge it can bring: We can be aware of the past and future as well as the present, aware of our own goals and intentions and the moods and attitudes of others, aware simultaneously of factors operating on many different levels. The knowledge we need to be successful in our work depends on learning to cultivate this awareness.

Awareness activates the dynamic qualities of the senses and the mind. It allows vision to take form, lets us establish clear goals, and invites the knowledge to accomplish those goals. Knowing what is important and valuable, awareness cares.

Like light shining in space, awareness reveals interconnections: Seeing both the details and the broad perspectives, it lets us predict, plan, analyze, organize, and focus. As the conductor and director of experience, awareness can guide the powerful energy of mind to accomplishment. Like a sculptor carving an image out of clay, it can shape what we do to produce results.

Awareness of Awareness

When we first begin to perform a task, we direct awareness to the activity at hand, but within just a few short minutes much of our attention is drawn into inner dialogues, images, concepts, and memories. Unrelated trains of thought start up and attract awareness to them. Images and memories pop up, float into the air, and disappear, like bubbles blown by a child, taking with them the awareness we have invested in them. At the back of the mind, a distant noise, fuzzy and distracting, also pulls attention away. Soon we may forget what we were doing and turn to something else. Even if the press of business pulls us back, our attention will lack the focus, sharpness, and clarity that come from being fully present.

When the mind loses focus, we do not realize that we are not aware; in fact, at such times we do not even know what awareness means. Never aware that anything is wrong, the mind zigzags back and forth or wobbles from place to place like a drunkard trying to walk. Externally we may be sitting in one place and working on one thing, but internally our mind is divided and dreamy.

Unaware of awareness, we are unaware of being distracted, unaware of the consequences of our actions, unaware of our lack of purpose. Conflicting thoughts and endless dialogues steal away our time and energy, exhausting us at a subtle level. When we receive tangible evidence that we have not accomplished very much, we cannot understand why; after all, we have been busy the whole time. But what is happening is not mysterious. We appear to be awake and active, but the most vital part of us is actually asleep.

When awareness is undeveloped, how can we be successful and productive? Lazy and undisciplined, mind starts off floating like a jellyfish, but soon it turns into a crab, possessed by resentment, anger, greed, jealousy and other negative emotions.

From within this narrow perspective, there is little light and little relaxation. We may think valuable thoughts, but we are not able to put them into action. The body becomes constricted and the senses and thoughts grow heavy and dark. Accustomed to listening to inner dialogues and attracted to mental images, we cut off direct sense experience and lose contact with our own natural intelligence.

The more we rely on what we see from this perspective, the more we create reasons to explain why it has to be that way, and the more real and true our reading seems to be. Soon we have established fixed limits on what we can do and accomplish. As this conclusion passes into consciousness, it dominates whatever positive thoughts and attitudes may arise. Since others share our perspective, they are quick to offer their sympathy and understanding, reinforcing our belief in our limited options and capacity.

When we have not trained our awareness, we cannot separate ourselves from these endlessly re-peating patterns of thought. Without being aware of our awareness, we have no access to a reality beyond the contents of what we are thinking. We cannot recognize or communicate anything other than what the shifting stream of thought allows. Unable to act on a deeper inner knowledge, we become isolated and weak, and the self-defeating quality of our isolation stimulates still more isolation.

This unending circular karmic pattern, burdensome and hopeless, is what the Buddhist tradition calls samsara. Living in samsara is like having an itch that never goes away. We scratch, but it does no good. The itch is everywhere—in our mind and body, thoughts and feelings. Whether we feel irritable and defensive, commit ourselves to seeking out pleasure or retreat into dullness, we are responding to a feeling of dis-ease and frustration. Perhaps our hopes and expectations soar momentarily at the prospect of a new job, a new relationship, or a new possession, but the old patterns soon recur, and our spirits sink once more.

Instead of condemning ourselves to these negative cycles, we can learn to train awareness. We can look clearly at our negative patterns and use knowledge of these patterns to wake up to our positive potential. We can use awareness as a medicine to heal dissatisfaction and cultivate enjoyment and deeper knowledge in our life and work.

The human spirit loves to explore freely and to fulfill its possibilities. We can tap into this dynamic adventurous force and let it empower us to prosper and achieve our goals. Work itself can be the vehicle for developing awareness, and awareness in turn can guide us toward success in our work.

Focusing Awareness

We tend to think that being aware comes naturally, like knowing how to walk or run. But just as our ability to move can be refined and trained through sports or dance, so our ability to be aware can be strengthened, exercised, and taken to higher levels. When we do not train awareness in this way, we are wasting a precious resource, like someone who has a grand piano in the living room but uses it only to pick out tunes with one finger.

We often associate awareness with a background sensitivity such as we experience while driving a car: a seeing in all directions that is like a three-dimensional halo to consciousness. When we first begin to train awareness, however, it is much more effective to look to the aspect of awareness that 'focuses on' or 'pays attention to'. As focus improves, the panoramic aspect of awareness increases naturally.

In training awareness to focus, we need at first to be as constantly watchful as a shepherd tending his flock. Otherwise thoughts, ideas, memories, images, and emotional dramas will wander aimlessly about and draw awareness to them. As we become more familiar with awareness, we do not need to exercise this same degree of vigilance, for awareness has a built-in reminding quality that will bring mind back to its object. Like a bee attracted to the pollen of a beautiful flower, awareness may fly away, but it keeps coming back.

Exercise 9   Keep It Simple

To cultivate a light, focused awareness in your work, start with a simple, short task and see if you can be aware of what you are doing from beginning to end—directly present in your own experience. If attention begins to slip away, gently bring it back. When you complete one task, do another. Every day and every hour, the opportunity to practice in this way is available.

Exercise 10   Working and Walking

A simple way to cultivate awareness is to focus on the activity of walking. Just as we walk from one place to another and do not notice how we get there, so we work to get something done and do not contact the experience of working. If we develop more awareness in walking, it will transfer to working.

Practice being aware of the activity of walking during the day. You will find that rushing about tends to diminish awareness, so it is best to begin by walking slowly. As you focus, you can develop a gentle sense of presence that makes you enjoy walking.

Once this enjoyment is activated, you can move quickly and still remain aware, opening the senses to what is going on around you. You will become more sensitive to the tendency for mental projections to take over awareness. As this sensitivity expands, see if you can consciously exercise it in your work.

Exercise 11   Developing Presence

This exercise can be done when driving a car or doing work with your hands. As you work, sense the body, starting at the top of the head and gradually letting attention move throughout the body. Once you are more aware of the body as a whole, see if you can bring the various sensations into balance. Notice where there are blockages, or where energy seems especially intense. Based on this balanced presence, focus in particular on the movement of the hands. Let this sensing expand into a more global awareness, so that the mind and the whole body are present together.

Expanding Awareness into Wholeness

By developing our ability to stay focused on what we are doing, awareness leads naturally into concentration and helps to stimulate energy. Together, these three resources—awareness, concentration, and energy—build the foundation for success. When we learn to promote their interplay, we set in motion a positive dynamic that leads to satisfying accomplishment, time after time.

Training in Concentration

Concentration is the quality of continuity or holding power: the ability to stay with the focus awareness chooses without becoming distracted. It merges awareness and gut-level energy, channeling thought and action toward a purpose and result. Through concentration, we gain the ability to penetrate experience with incisive intelligence and clarity.

Everyone knows the importance of concentration, and most of us may assume that we do our work with all the focus and concentration we need to succeed. Although we may notice that our focus is often interrupted by scattered thoughts or images or concerns, we tend to think this is natural. But imagine how much more we could accomplish if we could focus without interruption. What would we do with this extra productivity and effectiveness?

A mind that lacks concentration is like a tape recorder, taking in experience without determining what is important. For a while the mind may focus on the task at hand, but when distractions come up or emotions turn elsewhere, the mind follows. It responds mechanically to whatever thoughts or images our passing concerns or fancies generate, with no ability to set its own course.

Concentration is directed by awareness; without the guidance of awareness, concentration is like a firefly whose light flickers only briefly. As the carrier for the 'gathering together' quality characteristic of knowledge, awareness gives shape and coherence to what we are doing and guides concentration to focus until it burns with a steady intensity.

Drawing on Energy

To complete their work, awareness and concentration need energy, the dynamic power that enlivens experience. Flowing as the feeling of vitality and wakefulness, energy fuels our actions, empowers our senses and thoughts, and makes experience vivid.

Awareness can balance and direct the energy available to us, feeding it into concentration instead of letting it slip into emotionality and useless thoughts.

When this interplay has been activated, the mind can function at a whole new level.

We could think of awareness as the driver, concentration as the vehicle, and energy as the fuel that gets us where we want to go. Using these three resources together, we can define our work clearly, direct attention as needed, set targets, and move steadily to meet our goals, shaping our intention and intelligence toward a diamond-like intensity.

As we gain familiarity with the interplay of awareness, concentration, and energy, we will find that different combinations are suitable for different types of work. By observing and experimenting to see which are the best combinations for particular tasks, we can begin to learn more about their interconnections and make subtle adjustments that make us more effective. For example, while some kinds of work require a narrow focus, others need a broad perspective, and some call for a combination of both. Writing in a quiet environment, we can focus purely on the ideas and words before us; doing welding several stories up, we need to develop a broader kind of concentration.

Again, some jobs require soft energy and some need intense energy. To control powerful machinery like a jackhammer, energy must be both stable and powerful. Mental work or graphic design also calls for stable energy, but with a softer intensity. Similarly, when we make an initial plan for a project, a good sketch may be all that is needed to start the creative process. When it is time to refine the plan, however, we need a very precise and cutting awareness that carefully delineates each detail in sequence.

Developing Focus

A strong and steady focus will integrate awareness, concentration, and energy naturally. Remember that this focusing does not have to be a forceful act: You can proceed gently, sensitive to whether you are staying connected to your experience and your work from moment to moment. The results will manifest quickly in the quality of what you do and the results you get, giving you positive feedback that helps you stay on track.

Initially, focusing is a separate activity that we bring to our work, but gradually it becomes inseparable from the work itself. We are in contact with the tools we use, the materials we handle, and the goals we are working toward. Sensitive to the moods and needs of those we interact with, we develop a 'feel' for what we are doing. We discover that each type of work has its own texture and rhythm. Attuned to this inner form of work, we come to know what we are doing in a direct and immediate way. Awareness opens up, concentration holds the direction steady, and energy flows smoothly. We begin to enjoy a creative exchange with our experience that stabilizes and deepens our effort.

If the reality of the way you work seems far removed from this description, look to see how your activity lacks focus. To cut through the superficial level where you may seem to be busily working, ask whether you are getting good results. If the answer is no, a flood of excuses and explanations may come up. Try not to be drawn into this level of storytelling, which is designed to drain off energy and prevent anything from changing. Instead, appreciate the clarity that comes when you acknowledge what is going on. Now you may see elements in your work that you overlooked before: the needless busywork, the duplication, the way that you shuffle papers without really seeing them and talk around subjects without ever getting to the main point.

Exploring how well you focus will lead you to the way your mind operates. An unfocused mind is more interested in satisfying its own needs and desires than in dealing with what needs to be done. It may be able to concentrate for a while by relying on fear or jealousy or other forms of emotionality, but this concentration is not grounded in gut-level energy or guided by awareness, and it soon slips away.

When you discover that you are not focused, look closely: Can you see how the mind shifts and slides? How it dances and entertains itself? How it counsels the easy way and looks for compromises? Remember that time is slipping away, and let this thought inspire you to clarity.

By exploring the patterns of an unfocused mind—becoming aware of our lack of awareness—we automatically increase our awareness and become more focused. As we reactivate our focus again and again, we eventually discover in our focusing a special relaxation, a pool of positive energy that gives strength to concentration and feeds back into expanded awareness. When we feed this energy into our work, it becomes increasingly available. We may be amazed at how much we can accomplish.

Exercise 12   Focusing on Focusing

For the next week, cultivate a light, steady focus in whatever you do. Be aware of when you are focused and when you lose your focus. Note the times and conditions when your concentration is especially good. At the end of each day, note your observations. Review them at the end of the week, looking for patterns.

Exercise 13   Touching Work Directly

Explore the 'feel' of two different kinds of work that you do regularly. Can you contact a texture in the work? A rhythm? A shape and form?

Positive Cycle of Accomplishment

Awareness, concentration, and energy support one another in a positive cycle of accomplishment. Awareness brings in concentration; concentration brings in energy. Mindfulness brings in awareness; the senses bring in mindfulness; presence activates the senses; fullness of being abides in presence. As awareness and concentration increase and energy is stimulated, we see the value of being fully present in time and of integrating the energy of the mind with the steady flow of experience through the senses. Awareness brings us knowledge, concentration guarantees that opportunities are not lost, and energy fuels our progress. Friends, guides, and protectors, these three resources allow us to awaken our creativity and intelligence.

As the arena for this interplay, work transforms our theoretical understanding of this dynamic into direct personal insight that we can implement effectively no matter where we are or what we are doing. We need no special training or guidance to use work in this way, no expensive technology, complicated methods, or sophisticated theories about organizations or management. We can demonstrate for ourselves that awareness, concentration, and energy let us take charge of our work and move toward success.

Awareness, concentration, and energy are refined through a precise process of cultivating, strengthening, expanding, and maximizing. The more we use them, the more effective they become. We learn to train the mind, operate the senses, and make use of thoughts to direct our efforts and organize our intention. We become more stable, strong, and responsive, more confident and open.

Filled with a delicious sense of well-being, we can point to our achievements and see for ourselves the quality of our experience. Coordinating our creativity and imagination with the beauty of the senses and the active dynamic of the body, we can claim the full riches of our human inheritance. In this magical way of being, there is no limit to how much we can achieve.

Exercise 14   Work Training

Sit quietly and reflect on your abilities as they are expressed in your daily work. What are your strengths? What are your weaknesses? Consider practical skills and technical knowledge as well as attitudes, understanding, energy, and emotional stability. Now ask yourself what special opportunities your work gives you to develop greater knowledge and improved skills in each of these areas. How can you take full advantage of those opportunities?

After a period of quiet reflection, make an entry in your journal on the same themes. Return to these questions from time to time as you work with this book, and occasionally review your journal entries. What shifts do you see?

Exercise 15   Discovering Clarity and Ease

Begin to explore Exercise A on p. 243. Practice daily for at least a week. If you find the practice useful, continue for a month or more.

Pyramid
of Knowledge

To help identify awareness, concentration, and energy in action, we can classify three different levels of their operation. Becoming familiar with these levels strengthens our ability to observe what we are doing as we work, supports our ability to focus, and helps us to increase our efficiency and effectiveness.

First Level

At the first level, all three resources are low. We are not very aware of what we are doing and are prone to make mistakes. The ability to focus is weak, and the quality and quantity of the work we produce are relatively low. Our efforts to concentrate are only sporadically successful, and this is considered natural. Much of our energy is channeled into emotions and excuses, leaving little fuel for positive accomplishment. Locked within emotional patterns and internal dialogues, energy itself grows tired. Imbalances of energy in the body and mind lead to weariness, sluggishness, scattered focus, and possibly illness. We are easily discouraged; work is often stressful. We sense time passing but do not know where it went.

At this level, we do not recognize awareness, concentration, and energy in action. However, we may be aware that we are not as successful as we could be, or notice that we are having difficulty concentrating, or that our energy keeps falling off.

If we resolve to challenge this way of being, we can develop greater sensitivity to awareness, concentration, and energy. The key is to start with awareness; then we can identify and differentiate each resource in turn, locate it in our experience, see its specific function and purpose, and recognize how each supports the others. At this level, we improve by focusing on increasing our productivity and skills. As our skills grow, we are able to help others more effectively. Still, our discipline is not strong enough to make fundamental changes. Even if we do make special efforts, our lack of awareness means they will not be reinforced.

The three tables on the following pages point out how low levels of awareness, concentration, and energy shape the quality of our lives and the worth of our activity.

Second Level

At the second level, we make a firm commitment to developing greater awareness, concentration, and energy. As we learn to focus awareness, the quality of work improves, our output increases, and we grow

Low Awareness

QUALITIES

lack of focus
lack of global understanding
lack of specific understanding

STRUCTURES

inner knowing suppressed
appreciation dulled
creativity and vision limited
organizing principle: confusion

PATTERNS

lack of conviction and direction
doubt and hesitation

SURFACE MANIFESTATIONS

accepting routine
using one-dimensional guidelines
reliance on reasons and theories
free play for excuses
short-term thinking

RESULTS

superficial answers
problems without solutions
broader possibilities excluded
spontaneous insights fade

Low Concentration

QUALITIES

lack of focus
disconnectedness

STRUCTURES •

direct contact with experience suppressed
interest fails to deepen
no continuity
organizing principle: grasping

PATTERNS

accepting diluted experience
not penetrating confusion

SURFACE MANIFESTATIONS

sporadic effort
obsessive concern
easily confused
easily agitated

RESULTS

work not thorough
no completion
results inconsistent
short of time
scattering
opportunities not noticed

Low Energy

QUALITIES

lack of commitment and motivation
lack of determination

STRUCTURES

lack of caring and feeling
gut energy not available
organizing principle: aversion

PATTERNS

holding back
passivity mistaken for happiness
sensory experience pale
no inspiration
feedback dull

SURFACE MANIFESTATIONS

sluggish and plodding
rejecting new possibilities
refusal to commit to goals
tasks appear overwhelming
boredom

RESULTS

no achievement
lost opportunities
lack of real enjoyment and deep satisfaction
wasting time
idle activity

more motivated and energetic. We become more aware of what we are doing, sensing, and thinking, and learn to be more present in our work. Instead of encouraging excuses, daydreams, and thoughts or becoming lost in confusion, we learn to be aware of the present *within* concentration. We *become* the awareness that focuses and the energy that supports concentration. Concentration supports one unified mind working with its object. Whatever we hear or see, imagine, or fantasize cannot interfere with this strong focus.

Once this concentration has come into play, awareness guides it to assure that it continues. Simultaneously, awareness monitors energy, directing it into concentration, keeping concentration dynamic and alive. Work is transformed into a dynamic challenge that expresses our own values—a means of putting into practice who we are and what we choose to be. This way of working moves toward a future in which we can greatly benefit others and leave a legacy for those who will follow us.

Although we have made significant progress, concentration at this level remains inconsistent. We may be able to concentrate well in the morning, but fall off in the afternoon or evening; we may be easily bothered by noise or small interruptions. The quality of concentration is also still somewhat loose and shallow. Thoughts, memories, and worries about the future pop up and disturb its continuity.

Energy likewise flows only intermittently. Enthusiasm and enjoyment cannot be sustained, and the flow of energy in the body becomes blocked at different places, erupting into impulsive action or sinking into cloudiness and numbness. Because the flow of energy is somewhat thick and heavy, the quality of sense experience is not refreshing and dynamic.

The way to move beyond this level is by improving the quality of energy. Clarifying awareness and balancing the emotions lets energy move more freely through the body centers, and its quality becomes clear, clean, and vital. Unhealthy physical and mental conditions clear up; stress, confusion, and feelings of numbness are relieved, and we no longer feel needy. As a direct result, awareness becomes sharper and the quality of concentration more refreshing and deep. Focused concentration supports stable energy, which in turn fuels concentration and allows for further refinement. Focus becomes perfected in full concentration: Distractions cease, and we learn what it means to control time. Positive feelings expand into unlimited appreciation of life's abundance and beauty, and we move toward greater competence.

The growing success that comes at this level gives our energy a positive, inspirational quality free of restrictions. Enthusiastic about being engaged in work and perfecting our abilities, we sharpen our skills and discover new challenges. We can easily learn new disciplines.

Third Level

At the third level, awareness, concentration, and energy are fully integrated. Awareness is wholly absorbed in work, and concentration naturally supports powerful resolve, so that energy flows without interruption. At this stage, concentration actually transcends ordinary mind to arrive at full contemplation. The sign of this contemplation in action is that there are no mistakes.

At this level, all activity exhibits the beauty of art, the enjoyment of play, and the satisfaction of service. Our dreams and imaginations are fully applied in our work and become a means of refining our higher goals. The greater our experience with this way of working, the higher the goals we can set.

As contemplation continues, it becomes meditation. Its open intensity releases energy and vision, revealing new knowledge and fresh awareness. Awareness deepens into complete insight, and visions of knowledge take form and can be skillfully developed, manifesting in successful action.

Pyramid of Knowledge

As awareness, concentration, and energy develop through these stages, growing sharper and more skilled through application, their active interplay builds a pyramid of knowledge. At the summit, where the power of awareness merges with the power of energy and the power of concentration in a single point, knowledge wakes up fully. This is the inner meaning of skillful means: Waking up to the Body of Knowledge, so that we can embody in our work the abundant treasures brought forth from the marriage of wisdom and action.

PART TWO

Structures for Accomplishment

Paying Attention

The methods for increasing productivity and effectiveness that we generally rely on today depend heavily on specific techniques and technologies. Theories of management and productivity start from an underlying view that sees organizations as mechanisms or organisms in which each person has a specific role to play, and attempt to maximize the organization's human resources by establishing rules and policies that regulate the relations of the parts to the whole.

While these methods are effective on one level, they tend to treat people as known, fixed resources. Despite programs to teach employees new skills, new ways of learning, and new attitudes, there is little sense that each individual within the organization can develop his or her inner resources and creativity.

The skillful means approach is quite different. It is based on activating the power of knowledge that each of us possesses. Because working with skillful means develops the qualities of the mind, it allows us to improve our work at a level that goes deeper than specific techniques. We can be confident in our ability to control technology, no matter how sophisticated it becomes, and to use work for our own benefit and the benefit of others.

Awareness in Action

The key to this inner development is activating awareness as we work—learning how to pay attention. By cultivating mindfulness and maintaining focus through awareness, we can heighten our energy and motivation, expand our knowledge, maximize our use of time, and enjoy the profits from our efforts each day.

Being aware has a light, unforced quality. Awareness sees and does without concern or pressure, without worry or guilt. Each time we realize that awareness is caught up in thoughts and images, we can gently return our focus to our work. When we leave something unfinished, let an opportunity pass by, or fail to meet a goal, we can use the opportunity to ask with care and sensitivity what is going on.

Looking ahead and taking care of things on time, awareness protects us from surprises and emergencies. Always on the alert for more effective ways of acting, awareness leads us in the right direction, showing us how to balance priorities, focus on what is important, make good decisions, and accomplish something of value.

Work is a mirror of awareness, and the quality of our awareness sets the tone for how we work. As awareness becomes brighter and sharper, we de-

---

Daily Checklist

Start the day by reflecting on the key questions below, adding your own to the list. Remember to check back at the end of the day: How well did you do?

What are my priorities for today?
How will I focus my awareness?
How can I measure my success?
Who is depending on me?
What am I forgetting or ignoring?
What is cloudy or foggy? Being covered up?

---

velop a better understanding of the purpose of our work. We gain clarity about what we believe in and stand for, why we are working, and what meaning our work has. Building on this understanding, we can plan and set goals effectively. Awareness lets us think independently, setting priorities, sorting through them, and being sure to achieve them. When awareness operates at this global level, attention to the details of work comes naturally, for this is how we express our commitment and assure good results.

A simple aid to awareness is to carefully prioritize and schedule our time. For example, we may decide that today we will not work on project A at all, but will complete half of project B, a key step of project C, and one small aspect of projects D, E, and F. Taking control of our work in this way supports positive results. We will not forget important matters or let smaller concerns slide, and we can guard against becoming overwhelmed or drained by guilt, worry, resentment, or resistance. We work with a light, enjoyable quality that builds confidence.

Because awareness sharpens our faculties, it facilitates better working relationships, makes for sound business judgment, and helps us clarify financial and legal issues as well as schedules and plans. We can make sure that decision-making and communication are timely; that safety precautions, legal filings, and machine maintenance are scheduled and carried out in a timely and effective manner. Such timeliness helps to create a clear, orderly, and wholesome environment in which awareness can be further refined.

When we first focus on awareness in our work, we associate it with the head: planning, watching out for details, and so on. Later, however, we find that awareness is also intimately connected to the senses, the whole body, and the special knowledge of the heart. When the eyes are aware, we see small shifts and openings; when the nose is aware, we smell out trouble spots; when the voice is aware, we sense the impact we are having on others. Fully aware with all of our senses, we do not allow ourselves any excuse for not having knowledge.

Refining the Particulars

Paying attention moves to a deeper level of caring when we extend awareness to every aspect of our work. The appreciative awareness that enjoys the fragrance of a flower or sunlight shining on trees is the same quality of mind that notices all the particulars of daily activity.

When we are caught up in the pressures of work, the tension we feel may trick us into thinking that appreciation for the small details is a luxury we cannot afford, but this is not so. Being fully present in the moment, open and responsible, is a vital part of protecting our inner resources and the quality of our work. When we are aware at every level, we notice what needs to be done. Then we can act on what we see, following through to guarantee results. If we try to forcibly control our situation by narrowing our focus and ignoring what is going on around us, we sow the seeds for difficulties later on and undermine our own abilities.

One way to refine awareness of particulars is to practice fast feedback. Giving a message or getting a piece of information can usually be handled quickly. Turning the small things around right away and responding to others without having to be asked or reminded uplifts everyone's energy and helps to avoid problems and delays. In this context, impatience can be an effective resource: The quality of frustration that arises when we face the innumerable small details of our job can be forged into a tool we can use to 'just do it': just write that letter, just place that order, just make that phone call, just close that window. Taking care of something small quickly makes sure that it stays small.

Caring about every aspect of our work also lets us open the focus of awareness so that our view expands beyond our immediate and local concerns. If we combine this broad focus with strong concentration, we can organize time and space with discipline and precision so that each task, large or small, will have a place and an occasion.

Truly caring about details helps us channel our energy into creative work instead of emotionality or distractions. This shift not only supports the growth of awareness; it also opens up large reserves of vitality that enable us to persevere in the face of obstacles. We can remind others and ourselves of what needs to be done in a light and cheerful way and get back good results.

Controlling Waste

A good place to practice paying attention is in cutting back on waste. For example, anyone responsible for purchasing materials can make a careful estimate, allowing only a small margin for error, and then help regulate the work so that it stays within those boundaries. This approach develops discipline and care that affect every other aspect of the work. If we consider the consequences of wasting even one pound of steel, one inch of copper tubing, or a dozen sheets of paper, we can prevent small amounts of wastage from being multiplied many times over on large-scale projects. Alertness here will also sharpen our sensitivity to the patterns through which we are wasting our time and energy.

Because we have long considered this a land of abundance, we have only recently become sensitive to the issue of waste. It is helpful to remember that the materials we routinely discard in this culture would be considered valuable resources elsewhere. In other, less privileged lands, every sliver of beautiful fabric or fine paper, every metal scrap or rusty nail would be picked up and put to use.

To help encourage greater sensitivity to the issue of waste, we can reflect that when we waste materials, we are wasting the knowledge and effort of those who provided them. Just as the food on the dining room table arrives there through countless labors, so raw materials depend on the natural forces that made them, the machinery used to extract or refine them, and the complex web of transportation, communication, marketing, and sales that makes the economy function.

Perhaps the best way to focus on the issue of waste is to consider the real purpose of our work. Every dollar we misspend is not just wasted; it is subtracted from the money available for achieving our goals. For example, if we purchase just a little more than we need for a project to establish a 'comfort zone' for ourselves, we end up with scrap instead of money. We may find some use for the scrap, but in the meantime, the dollars that could have contributed to achieving our real goals are gone. And if the scrap sits idle, it becomes garbage that we must eventually pay to dispose of, either in money or in energy and time.

Paying attention to waste can expand into more efficient and economical ways of working. When we discover areas in which materials are routinely lost or misused, we can take the opportunity to heighten our caring and discipline. For instance, we can keep clear boundaries between work areas; we can protect boundaries between projects by careful records and calculations that prevent the casual flow of materials from one project to another. By being aware of every aspect of the process, on the lookout for possible flaws, and committed to making improvements, we can perfect our ability to use our resources well.

Countering Confusion and Forgetfulness

Paying attention promotes a 'no nonsense' approach to business that offers much more than cost savings. Seeing the hidden costs in each aspect of our work—in materials, time, or inner resources—helps to show us what we are getting back for our efforts and puts us more in touch with the reality of our work. We grow more willing to be present in our experience, to exercise awareness and relax into concentration. This discipline strengthens our ability to keep in mind what is important and to act on this vital knowledge.

The ability to use work in this way has special importance today, because our natural ability to pay attention is weakened by the circumstances of modern life. From earliest childhood, our minds are overstimulated with images, sights, and sounds. Constantly bombarded with sensory and mental overload, awareness grows cloudy. We lose the ability to see clearly in the present or project accurately into the future.

When we cannot sort through the barrage of thoughts and images in our minds, we pull back the energy of the gut and give way to emotionality. We fall naturally into a pattern of denial: I cannot see, I cannot understand, I cannot do. The more we choose to ignore what is happening, the more easily we forget what really matters to us, and the more our appreciation for experience diminishes. Opportunities slip by unnoticed, and we begin to be ruled by a sense of fear or anxiety that mirrors the sense of being overwhelmed. Often we describe these reactions in psychological terms—confusion, neurosis, dependency, emotional disorders—but the inability to bring real clarity into our awareness is a more fundamental cause.

The wish to be successful and accomplish something of value can be a powerful antidote to these patterns. Our strong motivation helps us recognize the importance of paying attention in our work, and we begin to foster the alertness and mindfulness that restore our natural intelligence and energy. As we see for ourselves the power that comes from really focusing the mind, we resolve to treat our awareness with the care it deserves.

Exercise 16 Holding on to What Counts

In the morning, memorize the three, five, or seven most important things you have planned for the day.

Let the list play in your mind lightly from time to time—more as a vision of the day than a rigid framework. This practice helps to keep awareness sharp and alert.

Exercise 17   Increasing Awareness

At the end of each hour, write down in five words or so what you have accomplished. Pay no attention to excuses and explanations; take a few seconds to make your report and then move on.

Exercise 18   Mental Notes

As you move around your office or work site, practice opening the senses wide and observing everything you pass. Once a day make a special tour, imagining as you do that you are moving through your own body. Look for potential trouble spots, making notes on each small thing needing attention that cannot be taken care of on the spot. At appropriate intervals, collect the notes and develop a plan for repairing, organizing, fixing, or cleaning whatever needs attention.

Exercise 19   Deepening Appreciation

Try expanding your awareness to encompass the history and background of your project or enterprise and the efforts of those who came before you. Look also at the positive results that come when your work is successful, tracing out as far as possible who will benefit and in what ways. Note the difference between appreciating these benefits and the sense of self-importance typical of daydreams about success.

Expanding awareness in this way opens the heart to a deeper level of caring and helps you see new ways to maintain and care for your work. This exercise is useful when you feel discouraged or frustrated.

Exercise 20 Momentum for Awareness

The commitment to developing awareness in our work depends on acknowledging the value of what we want to accomplish. Set aside time each day for a week to contemplate what is important for you in your work. Look at personal goals as well as the goals of your business or your specific job responsibilities. Writing in your journal, establish priorities and begin to map out a path to accomplishing them. The commitment that comes from developing vision in this way naturally elevates awareness and helps to sustain it.

Structures for
Accomplishment

At the beginning of any project or enterprise come vision, goal, and purpose, and the commitments we make to bring them into being. In the middle comes fulfilling our commitments through action. At the end is reflecting on what we have done and taking pleasure in our accomplishments.

For example, looking at our lives as a whole, we begin by growing up, completing our education, and starting to develop our livelihood. During these years we articulate our vision, determine our goals and purposes, and begin to manifest them in action. In the middle years the emphasis is on working, acting, and accomplishing—bringing our values into being. In later years we bring our efforts to completion, appreciating what we have done and rejoicing with deep satisfaction.

We can let this rhythm of beginning, middle, and end give shape to the working day. In the morning, we prepare for the day and start to work. During the day, we do the important things quickly, feeding each accomplishment into the next, dealing decisively with obstacles so that they do not interrupt the flow of the work. At the end of the day, we create as much closure as possible, cherishing our positive results so that we gain confidence and can challenge ourselves to accomplish more. Even if the content of our work is similar from day to day, or if we are working with problems that are difficult to solve, we can complete each day with satisfaction and start each morning anew, with clear, fresh perceptions.

Through this simple structure, we can appreciate more fully the opportunities that work presents us. Each twenty-four-hour unit becomes a whole, rich with accomplishment, full of meaning and value.

Four Stages of Accomplishment

Almost any successful venture we undertake has four stages: preparing the foundation, starting into action, developing strength and getting results, and enjoying the fruits. Awareness, concentration, and energy can support success at every stage.

Preparing the Foundation   Whether we focus on goals that are long-range or short-range—what we plan to accomplish in our lives or what we expect to do in a day or a month—we need to create a foundation. The first step is to become clear on our aims, for otherwise our aspirations will remain vague and dreamy.

It is also important to evaluate our motivation. Are we sincere in setting our goal, or are we simply caught up in superficial excitement? It is easy at the beginning of an enterprise to become fascinated and

---

Four Stages of Accomplishment

Preparing the foundation
Starting into action
Developing strength and getting results
Enjoying the fruits

---

energized, but this enthusiasm soon gives way to confusion and discouragement, and the goal slips out of reach. If our motivation is not solid, it is better to adjust our goal accordingly.

Once we have made our intentions clear to ourselves, we need to prepare for effective action. For example, if we want to enter a field where we have little or no previous experience, we need to educate ourselves, identifying the key ingredients for success and researching and analyzing relevant data. We can find out how others set up similar projects, what problems they encountered, and how they overcame obstacles. We can reflect on our experience in other work and the lessons we have learned. Where our knowledge base is incomplete, we can seek additional information and consult with professionals.

Next we must consider what it will take in time and resources to reach our goal. Activating knowledge and awareness to create a realistic blueprint or map, we lay out the key steps so that the goal begins to come into focus as a real possibility. As we review our resources—people, money, facilities, equipment, and especially knowledge—we can identify specific targets to meet by specific times.

Since the process of traveling toward the goal will itself generate new knowledge, we do not necessarily need to make a comprehensive plan before getting started. When we know what steps must come first, we are ready to take action.

Starting into Action With the plans and preparations made, we can put our vision and goals to the test, exercising our intelligence and experience in action. Often obstacles emerge at this point. Fear and doubts may block our energy or lead us to waste time in overplanning or in daydreams of success. If we lose sight of the benefits of our vision, our enthusiasm and commitment may drain away. Negative trains of thought may block our motivation, overpowering the forward-going energy of waking up and acting, so that we put off what needs to be done. Such procrastination turns us away from our vision and purpose and commits our energy to worry and excuses. Soon our gut-level energy fails us. We are left discouraged and frustrated, uncertain that our vision can materialize.

The decisive response to this negativity comes when we simply get up and do something. Action that takes a long time to get results is not suitable; we need to do some small thing—whatever is appropriate—that will encourage us instantly and help us awaken fresh and wholesome energy.

Having taken one step, we can take another. Starting into action fosters our willingness to act and encourages us to do more. Soon we see through the obstacles, remember the internal and external resources available to us, and wake up to our opportunity. Then opportunity itself can conduct awareness and concentration to the task.

As we achieve our first goals, we see new connections that make it easier to move toward the next set of goals. This pattern repeats itself: The feedback from each step gives us more knowledge to organize later steps more effectively. As our vision begins to come into reality, it extends further into the future, making it easier to set priorities and make good decisions. The path grows clearer and the vision brighter with each step, and we can make real progress in our chosen direction.

Each new task we take up offers many opportunities to challenge our limitations and apply our knowledge. We can guard our energy, goals, and resources by planning well, making schedules, and setting deadlines. We can cultivate light, positive energy that refreshes the mind and senses and protects us from exhaustion when the pace becomes hectic and busy. When our motivation flags, we can build our confidence by appreciating our successes and seeing our failures as opportunities for growth.

Developing Strength and Getting Results Without results, even the best intentions do not have much worth. But once we are underway and really producing something, each step encourages us to do more. Each time we accomplish a goal, we gain confidence, as well as knowledge that improves our skills and abilities.

The inner dynamic of success is based on linking awareness and energy through accomplishment that shows up in time. This interplay gives rise to a special intimacy that lets us continue to care about what we are doing. In turn, our caring carries the insight of awareness to the willingness of our gut-energy. Attuned to the flow of time and expressing it in our actions, we experience the same rich satisfaction that inspires the artist or the successful entrepreneur.

This natural balance between practical accomplishment and founding inspiration is a key to the benefits that work has to offer. The direct link between getting results and spiritual values allows us to bring true fulfillment into everyday life.

A focus on getting results may seem far removed from our usual sense of personal development or gratification, which is strongly linked to psychological concerns and personal desires. But this is really a matter of attitude. When results come from cutting through our personal obstacles and negative patterns, spiritual growth, personal satisfaction, and practical accomplishment are unified.

The kind of obstacles that cut our energy and lead us to postpone action at the beginning of a project may well reoccur at later stages, as new frustrations and obstacles block our path. Such reactions may be especially strong just before a project comes to completion, almost as though we feared success or were hesitant to turn to the next challenge. Most of us can deal with a certain level of difficulty, but eventually we reach a critical turning point—the 'last straw'—and go into a protective mode. We build our doubts and concerns into walls of resistance, confirming that we cannot go further. We offer up reasons, excuses, and emotions, and activate various mechanisms designed to dull us to what is happening until it is too late.

The best and most direct way to meet this challenge is simply by getting results. When we are moving ahead with our plans there is no time to indulge in excuses or fall prey to confusion, nor is there any need to do so. We are too busy dealing with the present to get involved with past regrets or future worries. We are getting a steady return on our investment of energy, enjoying the results we achieve and reinvesting them toward our ultimate goal.

Work at this level is deeply interesting. It supports awareness by uniting all parts of our experience; it supports concentration by linking our efforts dynamically to results; it supports energy by allowing awareness to manifest its caring in time. This way of working may not always lead to success, but ultimately it encounters no obstacles. The dynamic of knowledge it puts into operation is more powerful than any of the limits that ordinary mind imposes.

Enjoying the Fruits As our goals begin to materialize, the fruit of each moment gives us direct pleasure. We can cultivate this enjoyment, appreciating it and feeding it back into our work, rewarding ourselves and stimulating our motivation to do even more in the future. This positive cycle becomes the basis for greater enthusiasm and creativity in whatever we undertake next.

Success in our efforts allows us to see clearly the benefit of working with skillful means. If we let this understanding sink in, it will enter into every moment of our experience, alerting us to new opportunities and deepening our appreciation. We can find the kernel of concentration at the heart of each thought and the inexhaustible flow of energy that shapes each action. We do not have to cultivate the ego-inflating confidence that comes from identifying with our success, but can rely instead on the clear and fearless knowledge that comes from seeing the dynamic that supports accomplishment.

Enjoying the fruits of our accomplishment prepares us to work with even greater intelligence and enthusiasm in the future. If we are ready to take a more expansive view, it shows us that what we have accomplished is possible for others as well, and invites us to dedicate our work to helping others succeed and enjoy what they do. In this way our skillful means extends out into the larger world, helping to wake up all humanity.

Exercise 21 Morning and Evening Exercises

Each morning and evening for at least two weeks practice Exercises D and E in Tools for Change, pp. 248–49. Where you see progress, let it feed your energy and motivation.

Exercise 22   Challenging Dreaminess

If we spent time thinking "Someday I'll be rich," but had no clear plan for bringing this wish into reality, we would be fooling ourselves. Even if we spent the same time drawing up plans without ever getting underway, we would be undermining our own knowledge and intentions. This kind of wishful thinking supports a dreamy quality that prevents us from taking action to realize our aspirations. The alternative is to act. What small step can you take today to bring an important goal closer to reality?

Exercise 23   Mapping Goals

Try mapping out specific goals to achieve by a certain date: three months, one year, two years. Within each of these time segments, define specific intermediate short-range goals that will lead step by step to your larger aims. This process takes you gradually forward, building your vision into a path for solid accomplishment.

Refining a Plan
in Action

To be effective, a plan must include detailed strategies for achieving the goals it sets. In refining our plan at this level, we need the most precise picture possible. A written plan is essential to support the strength, vitality, and viability of our vision. Without it, any venture is likely to remain in the realm of wandering mind.

In making a plan, clarify the pathways to your goals from start to finish, considering the risks and what could go wrong. There are many good books on business planning that can help guide you. With steady concentration you can visualize each stage of the work and understand the complex interactions sure to arise as you swing into action. As the timing of each phase becomes apparent, goals can be set by the month, the week, and day by day.

Steps for Clear Planning

If you do not have much experience or training in this area, the suggestions that follow may help you in making a plan more precise. They come into play once you have completed two initial steps: setting goals and reviewing your resources. They apply most directly to small-scale production, but can be useful in a wide variety of projects.

Calculating Rates Calculating rates for different tasks lets you see more clearly what can be accomplished in a given period of time. Finding a measure for dynamic, high-level accomplishment will give you clear feedback as you work, so you can evaluate your results and see what needs to be improved. Some types of work are difficult to measure, but if you look at the specifics, you can usually find some element that can be quantified in terms of time. You can share your ways of measuring performance with others involved in the same work, so that everyone gets a clear picture of what is an acceptable target and is motivated to look for better techniques. Such clarity also supports steady concentration and energy.

Those with professional training or engaged in creative work may resist this approach, which is usually associated with factory piecework. But specific measurement penetrates vague ideas or stories about why work is going slowly and helps you see clearly how and where you are losing time. The idea that creativity cannot be rushed or that key factors affecting timing are out of your control can easily become excuses for turning a project into a comfortable nest and losing track of the guiding purpose of your action.

Coordinating Work in Time and Space After you have looked at each separate task, imagine the work flow as a whole, visualizing what will be needed and

> ### Five Steps for Daily Planning
>
> Set goals
> Review resources
> Calculate rates
> Coordinate the work in space and time
> Keep communication open and flowing

when. Diagrams and charts can be useful in showing how each aspect of the work connects to other aspects and in developing a system to track each part.

Coordinating a project for several people involves coordinating its various elements in time and space, so that one person or work group does not run out of work because another group is behind schedule. Planning ahead for each day, each week, and each month develops awareness of how money, materials, staff, machinery, tools, and vehicles will intersect. Buying plans and budgets let you pinpoint the right times to buy different goods according to project needs. Planning for different spaces clarifies specific needs, including materials, supplies, and inventories. At the same time, it develops the clarity and scope of awareness, stimulating better results in every area.

The aim is to avoid duplicating effort, wasting materials, redoing work, or creating stoppages. The more clearly you can visualize the flow of work and the knowledge, resources, and skills needed for each project through time, the better arrangements you can make. A written review of the details also helps to sharpen focus and clarify interactions.

This kind of coordinating requires distinguishing the major focus of the work from the minor but necessary jobs. Major tasks require steady energy and power, while minor tasks can be fit in around the edges. Such 'fitting in' requires good planning, a big picture of what is happening, and above all, strong motivation to keep the work moving without disturbing the main focus. The feedback that comes through this process strengthens concentration and promotes a smooth flow of energy, without blockages.

Keeping Communication Flowing Good project communication covers three areas: timing, knowledge, and energy flow. Communication on timing deals with such elements as work schedules, deliveries, and pickups. Communication on knowledge deals with plans, technical skills, emerging trouble spots, safety, and the general well-being of all involved. Communication on the energy level is less direct: It involves making sure everyone is aware of how the work is progressing, what the energy level is, where the blockages are, and what could be improved. Where is energy moving and where is it stopping? Is each person working at maximum capacity? Is there a sense of teamwork?

Feedback and follow-up throughout the day help to sustain focus and protect schedules, and create genuinely supportive energy. When you are coordinating a project, note what happens when you receive a new piece of information that affects the plan

---

Rule for Accomplishment

Pursue   Persist   Remind   Follow Up

---

for the day. Who needs to know this information? What needs to change? Be particularly aware of assumptions and attitudes that may impede communication. For example, are you assuming that other people already have this information, so that you do not need to tell them? Are you willing to make the effort to find out? Are you willing to be in the position of reminding someone? Remember this rule for accomplishment: Pursue, persist, remind, follow up.

Sometimes people think that communication requires many meetings and much talking, but talking can easily drain time and energy. To prevent this, it can be helpful before a meeting to circulate a memo that clarifies the purpose of the meeting and sets an agenda, listing the items that need action and making a preliminary schedule. Before meeting, ask yourself three questions: Do I have valuable ideas and clear information to share? Can I explain my views well? Can I communicate concisely?

Evaluating Progress

Pausing to examine your progress helps you to see what you have accomplished and what needs to be improved, both short-range and long-range. This process of evaluation is essential to the success of any enterprise, whether it is a commercial operation, the business of living your life, or managing your mind.

Your assessment is the yardstick by which to measure the next steps. When you make a one-year plan, look to see how you are doing after two to three months. On long-range plans, evaluate your accomplishments each year and in three-year increments. Give each project time to develop, and then see how it is doing, making necessary adjustments. At the same time, it is good to evaluate progress on a daily basis. See Exercise E, p. 249.

In making your evaluation—and particularly with regard to financial decisions—it is important to balance the two personalities of business. One is always advancing, needing new equipment, products, or people, while the other holds back, protecting the organization's resources. Before making a decision, look in a comprehensive way, mediating between the two approaches. Operating in this way prevents one person's view from dominating and lets you balance your own thinking. It shields the organization from harm, especially in times of quick expansion, while also guarding against stagnation.

If your evaluation suggests that the results called for exceed the capacity of the people or machinery available, be careful to question in a penetrating way, drawing on all the awareness and concentration you can muster. The following questions should be intensively explored: How can productivity be increased with present resources? Are there resources you are not using? How can you strengthen your secret resources: awareness, concentration, and energy? How can you improve your use of time? of space? How can the existing structure be changed or revitalized to open up more knowledge?

The process of evaluation does not have to be carried out only at specific times. Each day you can be thinking creatively about what can improve your particular business or project. For example, what government, professional, and community resources are available? What do experts recommend, and how can you get them more involved? Cultivate people experienced in various aspects of business, such as marketing, publicity, and customer relations. Encourage anyone who could help you, identifying their interests and skills. Follow up on leads and communications energetically, creating a positive momentum that attracts people, energy, and knowledge.

For each project, you can develop blueprints for improvement. How can you make a better product? How can you improve sales, communication, management, financing, or fundraising? What new forecasting tools can you generate? How can you be more efficient with people, energy, money, timing, quality control, management, coordination? Never stop asking fundamental questions or challenging the standard answers; never take a vacation from knowledge.

Problem-Solving

Because even the best plan cannot foresee all possible difficulties that may arise, problem-solving is an integral part of any successful project. Each

91

problem solved adds to our store of knowledge, while effective problem-solving itself can be a deeply satisfying challenge.

Problem-solving mind is like enjoyment mind— open and responsive to the present moment. Daily work offers numerous opportunities for problem-solving, and if we work willingly with these challenges, we can become a master of dealing with the unexpected, delighting in each new solution. Even when a problem at first appears to be overwhelming, we can be confident that if we face it squarely we will be able to work with it.

Get the Whole Picture The first step in problem-solving is to get a clear picture of what is going on. Awareness needs to know both the big picture and the details. We may need to focus on the difficulty for several hours or even several days, holding it strongly in our minds to pinpoint what is causing the trouble. Where in the work process does the difficulty first arise? How does it occur? We may need to look into fields that overlap our specific project, such as budgeting, purchasing, or transportation. Is lack of skill or poor timing involved? Is there poor communication or planning?

When difficulties arise, there is a strong tendency to quickly put forth our ideas, assign blame, or defend our position. If we can learn instead to relax the energy of frustration, we can allow more space for new ideas. If we listen sensitively to what the situation is telling us and give others time to share their

---

Four Steps of Problem-Solving

These four steps can be used to solve problems in almost any situation:

Get the whole picture
Pick a new direction
Build a roadblock
Establish consensus

---

knowledge, we will be more likely to penetrate to the roots of the problem and find a good solution.

Pick a New Direction The second step is to ask what adjustments can be made. Awareness needs to relate ideas to the practical realm, rethinking the situation from different angles. Concentrating on one possibility at a time, awareness tracks out each new possibility to see what might or might not be useful. What could be altered in the work process or the plan? What factors must remain the same?

Build a Roadblock The third step is to decide on a solution and act decisively to implement it. The best solutions encompass three factors: They are directly connected to the problem, they reflect willingness to change direction, and they maximize efficiency and effectiveness. A good solution is like a roadblock that directs us away from danger. When the situation reaches a turning point, the roadblock prevents us from taking certain paths of action and guides us toward our destination on a new path.

Establish Consensus The fourth step is agreement among everyone concerned. At this point any misunderstandings can be cleared up and the basis for the decision clearly communicated. Real consensus establishes a basis for the group to work together harmoniously to make the solution effective. Each person will be responsible for helping keep to the new direction, reminding others what is at stake and offering feedback so that additional adjustments can be made as needed. This step can create an irresistible dynamic that completely shifts the direction away from danger and toward positive results.

Exercise 24   Tracing Transformation

Reflect back to a time when a potentially dangerous situation you were involved in was transformed into something positive through a shift in direction. Write a narrative account of what happened. Can you discover in that situation the four steps of problem-solving described above? Based on your narrative, are there any other steps you would add?

Exercise 25   Dealing with Difficulty

Training in awareness can help us spot problems before they overwhelm us. If difficulties do turn into emergencies, however, there are practices that can help us keep clarity, focus on what needs to be done, and balance our energy. In this way we keep our best resources available to help us focus on the problem. For some useful exercises, see Tools for Troubled Times at p. 253.

Inviting
Responsibility

Whatever the nature of our work, we can expand its purpose and increase its challenge by using it as the vehicle to develop a deeper level of responsibility. Our success or failure—and the success or failure of the company or organization for which we work—ultimately depends on our willingness as individuals to be responsible. Taking responsibility naturally increases our level of understanding and caring, our degree of participation, and our commitment to protecting the results of our own efforts and the efforts of others.

Many people are willing to take responsibility for success, but few are willing to take responsibility for failure. When things go wrong, there is a strong tendency to look away or point at others. The boss blames the managers; the managers blame the workers; the workers blame the managers or one another; everyone blames the economy. But real responsibility does not make such distinctions. If we have set a goal and are willing to do what is necessary to achieve it, we take responsibility for whatever happens, using our mistakes and failures as stepping stones for growth.

Holes in the Fabric of Work

When we hold back from taking personal responsibility the results manifest as holes in the fabric of our work. From a distance what we do may seem solid, and as long as we focus narrowly on a particular role or task, this impression is confirmed. But from a broader perspective, the integrity of our efforts is undermined by our refusal to look at the welfare of the whole. There are the little jobs that everyone imagines someone else will do, the details no one wants to take care of, the daily tasks that are parked to one side. Such little holes grow bigger and bigger, until eventually the fabric tears. The supplies no one purchased create a delay that undermines a whole project, the letter no one answered blocks communication. Gradually trust between individuals is shaken, respect is lost, and working together becomes increasingly difficult.

How can these patterns be prevented? How can we fire up our motivation, act with more consistency and integrity, and strengthen our determination? The answer lies in taking responsibility for our work at a deeper level.

Take some time to reflect on the value of the work you are doing. Do you care about producing good results? Do you care about learning to develop your own abilities? If so, you will naturally want to participate more fully in your work, helping to protect the fruit of your efforts. You will move naturally toward assuming more responsibility.

If we care about our work, the actions we take daily will express caring. This is the most admirable consciousness: compassionate, virtuous, generous with its time and energy, and willing to face reality and do what is needed to get results. When we are responsible at this level, we make our time count, benefiting from each day and each hour.

Inspiring and Motivating

The first step in taking on greater responsibility is to motivate ourselves to respond positively to challenge. We can look for inspiring models in history or within our field and investigate their accomplishments and methods; we can study the successes of our co-workers and friends. We can support and encourage ourselves by appreciating our own efforts and our results. By developing clarity about which kinds of activity are truly productive and valuable and focusing our energy accordingly, we can call forth our best efforts.

As we plan our work, we can inspire ourselves with the thought of achieving our goals, imagining the benefits for ourselves and others. We can appreciate the value of each step along the way, preparing well so we gain confidence by getting good results. We can think ahead to the dynamic and the requirements of each upcoming activity, visualizing the obstacles and readying ourselves to meet them.

The confidence that comes from this way of working lets us put both our strong points and our weak points in perspective. When we make mistakes, we can challenge ourselves to learn from them; when we succeed, we can encourage ourselves to accomplish more. Appreciating each advance we make will strengthen our caring and commitment and add to our reserves of energy. We will soon learn to replace idle talk and wishful thinking with effective action.

Every day, every hour, we can practice readiness, foreseeing problems and taking precautions that will guard against difficulty. We can make allies and learn to improve our communication with everyone. We can learn to relax the mind and invite creativity, and we can practice deepening our knowledge through concentration.

As we learn to respond deeply and fully to whatever comes up in work, our competence expands. We are equipped to try new projects and accept new responsibilities, even if they fall outside the range of our experience. We may want to take on different kinds of work, challenging ourselves like a rock climber ascending unfamiliar peaks. Understanding how to generate and sustain our inner resources, we can be successful in whatever we do.

Penetrating Obstacles to Responsibility

Our natural intelligence is ready to respond to the challenges we face at work—only long-established habits hold us back. For example, we may feel over- whelmed at the thought of taking on more responsi-

Improving Motivation

Inspire and encourage yourself
Study inspiring models
Study successes: your own and co-workers'

Get results
Plan well
Make full effort
Focus on long-lasting accomplishments

Appreciate the outcome
View mistakes as an opportunity
Enjoy your successes

bility, or lack confidence in our ability to do something new. Perhaps we resent being asked to do more, or let fear tie our energy up in resistance. We may expect to be blamed or worry about disappointing others if our work is not successful or our efforts seem out of line. Or we may not want to give up the pursuit of the passing pleasures with which we have learned to fill our days.

Once we begin to take responsibility, seeing these patterns in ourselves can inspire us to change. No longer afraid to care, we experience in our own hearts the cost of wasting or misusing our talents and intelligence. We see how we cut ourselves off from new opportunities, choosing the easy and familiar way. We begin to appreciate the opportunity to awaken and develop awareness, concentration, and energy. In time we become compassionate supporters of our growing sense of responsibility. Each task becomes an experiment in skillful means—a way to transform our obstacles and to test and refine new knowledge.

It is true that we may have to work hard to make something happen or to protect what is important. We may face difficult problems and challenges. But in the end we will get results and gain wonderful satisfaction. Eventually we can enjoy the special joy of sharing our knowledge with others.

Stepping into Responsibility

Once we step into responsibility, we begin to engage our work more completely. Since we are intent on getting results, we take charge of planning, organizing, guaranteeing, and protecting the project, or else give our full support to those who are already doing this. Since we 'own' the work, our energy shifts readily to the heart level and the gut level. We open our eyes to what is going on and train ourselves to make the best possible decisions.

To take responsibility for the whole scope of a project or goal, we need to be aware of the available physical resources: people, money, land, buildings, equipment, inventory, and so on. We can think of these resources as the basic skeleton of our project, the solid foundation on which we can build.

Within the organization itself, we need to have an overview of the structure of responsibilities, including key systems such as management, finances, production, and sales. If we are starting an organization, laying these systems out clearly and defining responsibilities and duties is a vital step. We need to set priorities, determine locations for the work, and define task forces. Do we understand how different systems interact, how each system is controlled, and who is responsible for what? Only when these structures are clear to us are we ready to delegate responsibility.

Once the foundation has been built with care and is well-supported, we can focus on the core of our project. Applying awareness, concentration, and energy, we can set about transforming resources such as time, energy, money, and materials into beauty and benefits for others.

To encourage a broad understanding of the purpose and direction of the organization and develop individual skills and abilities, it can be very valuable for everyone to learn more than one aspect of the work. For example, a person with primary responsibility for one major job can also be made responsible for following up on several other projects and for handling various routine tasks on the side. Greater knowledge of how the organization works stimulates openness and receptivity and encourages people to learn faster, to cooperate with one another, and take on more responsibility. People become interested in learning more and exercise their creativity more fully. This approach also encourages each person to be alert to matters that fall outside the scope of his or her usual duties, and to protect the aims of the organization as a whole.

When we care deeply about the success of the projects we take on and support them with responsibility, integrity, and determination, we naturally develop the concentration and gut-level strength to work with each obstacle. Instead of covering up difficulties or preparing our excuses, we use our knowledge to bring to light whatever has been ignored or is hidden or unclear. Willingness invites responsibility, responsibility opens up awareness, and awareness opens up what is right and good.

Expanding Responsibility

Awareness gives us the knowledge we need to accept the challenge of each new task. Though we may not know exactly how to proceed, we view our not-knowing as an open field of unformed possibilities. We step willingly into the unknown, eager to stimulate our own creativity. We usually have at least some idea of where to start, and once we let our intelligence operate without fear and holding back, we can act like heroes, confident in our abilities, ready to innovate, explore, and experiment until we find the best way to proceed.

To prevent slipping back into being unaware, it is important to wake up awareness each day, encouraging ourselves, engaging each task directly, and accepting full responsibility for what we are bringing into being. This responsibility is not a burden, but an expression of our own loyalty to what we value.

Like parenthood, it is a natural part of our sensitivity, understanding, and caring, so well developed that we do not need to remind ourselves to be responsible. Our devotion to our work gives our lives integrity that is inseparable from deeper knowledge.

Dedication to this way of life arises spontaneously from within daily work. The way we work expresses our commitment to responsibility, and responsibility guides the way we work, conducting us toward knowledge. Aware that the future depends on the present, we link future to present like an architect creating a model of a beautiful building. Our caring expresses our integrity and commitment, and manifests naturally in fully responsible action.

Essential Knowledge

The willingness to be responsible guarantees that our knowledge of how to refine awareness, concentration, and energy will continue to develop. More basic than technical expertise, management training, psychology, or philosophy, this knowledge holds the key to combining positive enjoyment and accomplishment. It creates skillful avenues to success, manifesting in relaxed, precise gestures and clear and open communication. When we base ourselves in this knowledge, we radiate confidence and joy. Our heart is smiling, and our hands are willing to help.

Exercise 26   Cutting through Reasons

A. What are the reasons you habitually give for not being more deeply involved in your work? Write down the first five reasons that come to mind. What attitude underlies each of them?

B. The next time you turn down a job or a new responsibility, what reasons do you give? How do they connect to the list you made earlier?

Exercise 27   A Qualities Checklist

Prepare a list of the qualities called for in your present work. Which ones could you improve on? Pick one or two qualities and identify at least two steps you could take right now to initiate this change. Look back in a week: How did you do? Each time you take on new responsibility, you can make a list of the qualities needed and use it to stimulate learning in the same way.

Exercise 28   Taking Initiative

A. Think of a frustrating problem that affects some aspect of your work. If you were the sole person responsible for a solution, what plan would you make? In answering this question, take the time to make a realistic plan, even if it seems far removed from the reality of the situation.

B. Now consider the same situation in terms of the people actually involved. How could you motivate them to participate in solving the problem? Make a plan to achieve this result and act on it. Don't be discouraged if you encounter obstacles: Just incorporate them into your plan. Set a deadline to review your progress in two or three weeks.

Exercise 29   Taking Responsibility

Sit quietly and cultivate a relaxed ease in your body and mind. Then bring to mind an aspect of work for which you are willing to take on more responsibility. This could be a task or area you have neglected, or a new area into which you wish to expand. Make sure it is something that will challenge your abilities. Imagine it in detail, and picture yourself engaged in handling it. Continue until you have a clear sense of the requirements of the work and any new skills you will need to develop.

Then write down a brief description of what you wish to achieve by taking on this new responsibility, and set an initial timeline for accomplishment. Are you willing to commit to the actions you have outlined? If so, start in on them. After three months, review your progress, and make a commitment to apply everything you have learned since you started. At the end of another three months, review your progress, reflect on your mistakes, and make a commitment to begin sharing any new understanding with others.

Exercise 30   Becoming an Owner

Sit quietly and release tensions in your body and mind. Imagine your workplace—the outside of the building as well as the interior—and the people you work with. Picture yourself as one of the owners of this company or organization. Imagine that each dollar spent comes out of your pocket; that each ·success reflects the value of your personal vision and your ability to bring that vision to life. As you foster and cultivate this attitude, what feelings are evoked?

Note any negative reactions that arise from taking this perspective, particularly jealousy or resentment toward the 'real' owners, and look carefully at the judgments that underlie these attitudes. Can you set these negative reactions aside and use this point of view to develop an understanding that can free you from these limiting responses? Even though you may not receive the financial benefits and prestige of ownership, you may find there is something about the attitude of being an owner that brings rewards at a much deeper level.

For the next two weeks, carry this attitude with you as you begin your work and throughout the day. How does your perspective on the work change? How is your sense of responsibility affected? How does this way of thinking affect your actions?

Refining
Decision-Making

The best safeguard for good decision-making is to develop our knowledge as fully as possible. We can do this by continually working to awaken awareness: cultivating sensitivity to our situation, projecting forward in time, and allowing for the unexpected.

The more complex and sophisticated the project, the more it requires independent thinking and a penetrating questioning that challenges old assumptions. Although we can consult experts, we may need to play off one expert against another and research many alternatives before making a decision. In consulting with others, we can look for ways to measure the level of awareness and creative intelligence they are bringing to bear on the issues at hand. Do they know how to concentrate and apply their best understanding? Can they transmit clearly the knowledge that has been passed on to them? If not, what they have to say will probably not be very reliable.

In choosing a new course of action, devising practical tests or models can be an important way to identify and plan for potential difficulties. If we do not realize that a particular obstacle could arise, the shock when it suddenly manifests can multiply its negative impact many times over. For the same reason, it is important to consult with others who have experience that we can use to our advantage.

The real key to effective decision-making is seeing ahead in time. If we see problems coming, we can act decisively to avoid them. If we see an opportunity, we can prepare ourselves to take advantage of it. By looking ahead to the likely results of our actions, carefully thinking through each aspect of our situation and cultivating new sources of knowledge, we can guard our goals and commitments, better handle life's surprises, and protect against damaging mistakes.

Looking ahead allows us to plan intelligently, preparing well, gathering the necessary information, and making sure that each important point has been taken into consideration. One helpful practice is to visualize the effects of a plan or a proposed decision unfolding in the future. Another is to relax the mind and let sequences of complex details flow through it as water flows through a river canyon. Observing without becoming anxious or emotionally involved, we may see unexpected twists and turns up ahead.

Long-Range Thinking

Each decision we make will have both short and long-term effects. It is common to focus on the short-term results, particularly if we feel that we will be judged by immediate outcomes. But generally the more responsible course is to focus on the long-term effects, especially the expected benefits of our action.

We should learn to ask questions that throw such issues into sharp relief, not settling for vague answers from ourselves or from others. What will make our business healthy? What are the trends in our major markets? What effects will the action we are considering now have in twenty years? In a century? What will its impact be on other projects and goals that we are pursuing or that we value?

The failure to engage in such long-term thinking has led to serious difficulties in our society, and the more technologically advanced we become, the more true this will be. Initiating vast changes and attempting sweeping solutions without having the knowledge that can penetrate to the roots of our problems and predict the consequences of our actions, we have learned through painful experience what it means to operate without real awareness. It is almost inevitable that decisions made on this basis will not support us in achieving our goals.

A good example of the results of such decision-making, and one from which we can draw many valuable lessons, is the pollution of the environment that has gone on largely unchecked for most of this century. Today we know that we cannot continue to contaminate the earth, the oceans, the sky, and space with garbage and dangerous waste; we understand with new clarity that what happens in one place and time will have consequences that extend far into the future. Yet this knowledge has come too late to prevent real damage, and reversing the consequences of what we have done is proving a challenge of enormous proportions. It is difficult to pinpoint how these trends could have been identified and changed at an earlier time, but one point is clear: Our best protection against such policies is awareness that is both sharp and caring—ready to trace the consequences of our actions far into the future and to guide our course in a beneficial direction.

Dealing with Uncertainty

Often we cannot be certain where a particular course of action will lead, but this does not have to prevent us from making a start. We can take small steps to begin with, observing the results and building confidence. This confidence helps us to concentrate and to make contact with gut-level energy. Then awareness can expand, opening to new possibilities and giving us trustworthy feedback. Sometimes it takes only a brief experiment before we know enough to make a wholehearted commitment.

There are times when we have to make a decision knowing that we lack the broad experience and deep insight that would show us the best way to proceed. In addition to conducting a thoughtful analysis, we should take care at such times to relax our energy and calm the mind, so that we can develop greater sensitivity to our own moods and to the surrounding circumstances. It may also be useful to discuss our options with an experienced mentor who can help us clarify what is at stake and perhaps provide new perspectives and specific information that we had overlooked.

Although we may have considerable experience with attempting to assess the impact of external factors on our decisions, a more subtle and refined approach puts equal or greater emphasis on awareness of our own thoughts and emotions and those of others. The decision to develop this sophisticated knowledge is a turning point in our lives, for such understanding lets us take into account the consequences of each word, gesture, or action. It reveals a hidden dimension to our actions and our communications: a layer of intentionality and reactivity that has a profound impact on whether our choices will lead to success or failure.

Without knowing how to operate at this level, we are like a very near-sighted person trying to drive a car on the freeway: The risks are great. On the other hand, when we are sensitive to this inner dimension, we can make decisions with much more confidence. In today's global community, where the consequences of our actions may have far-reaching effects, it is particularly urgent to develop such clarity.

Facing Limits on Our Knowledge

Despite our best efforts, situations will still arise that are so unpredictable and delicate that we are unable to prepare in advance and have no models on which to rely in making our decisions. At those times, it is especially important to consult with colleagues and build consensus. Thinking and planning together, we can balance one another and help point to places where emotional reactions are obscuring clarity. We can make a mutual commitment to raise awareness to the highest possible level, and then decide.

In the face of uncertainty, the best response is usually to proceed with caution. If we act too quickly, we may find ourselves taking action we cannot afford or that bears only limited fruit or fosters undesirable qualities. Like someone operating unfamiliar equipment, we should be clear on the consequences before we act impulsively. By sorting things out carefully and preparing in a rational manner, we will not put our previous gains at risk.

Finally, it is important to acknowledge that whenever we have responsibility for making decisions we will also make mistakes. Actions that seemed right at the time often prove to have unforeseen negative consequences. However, this does not necessarily mean that they should be abandoned. Perhaps the difficulties that our decision brings are short-term; perhaps in the long run the benefits we had expected will manifest. As the results of our action begin to make themselves felt, we must continue to use our awareness fully to monitor each new development. Awareness supported by focused concentration and balanced energy will always be our best guide in deciding how to respond.

Even if a decision does prove to have been mistaken, we can benefit from getting clear on what went wrong and how. We can learn how to respond to similar situations in the future, and we may also learn something valuable about the limits of our own ways of making decisions. Whatever happens, we should reflect on the results in light of our long-range goals. A failure along the path of accomplishment can still be a valuable experience that supports our progress toward our ultimate aims.

Exercise 31 Probing the Past

A. Reflect carefully on a past decision that had negative consequences. Spend a few minutes recalling the sequence of events. Try to relive the situation, visualizing its particulars, looking for factors you may not have noticed in the past. Then write down answers to the following questions: How was the decision made? Who was involved? How carefully was the decision prepared and researched? What warning signals indicated trouble ahead? What attitudes, moods, or emotions influenced the decision? What was ignored? Seeing what you see now, how would you respond differently? What makes you think this response would be more effective? If new knowledge comes out of this exercise, let yourself taste its flavors fully.

B. In the same way, reflect carefully on a decision that had positive consequences. Does it feel different to conduct this inquiry?

C. Reflect on a shocking or surprising action by a co-worker or friend. Sit quietly and spend a few minutes recalling the action itself and the significant words, actions, moods, and gestures that led up to the action. Was the person communicating something that you or others did not want to hear or acknowledge? What was not communicated? What was ignored? Seeing what you see now, would you act or speak differently?

D. In learning from these and other past experiences, you can follow a series of four steps:

1. Recall the event fully.

2. Ask "What was ignored?"

3. Bring what was ignored then into full awareness now, with as much vitality and 'presence' as possible.

4. Visualize new knowledge being activated in the situation through your increased understanding.

You can repeat this sequence three or four times or until you sense there is no longer anything hidden. One indication that this is so may be that the outcome you visualize becomes harmonious and balanced; however, be careful not to force this result prematurely.

Exercise 32   Contacting Light

For readers who already have experience with methods for relaxing the mind and senses, this exercise can activate a more subtle awareness and bring innovative knowledge into decision-making.

Start by imagining space without light, dark and silent. Gradually a diffused light becomes visible and spreads throughout the whole of space. This light has no source and cannot be captured, but it illumines forms and shapes and can be seen and contacted by inner awareness. Let this awareness open into contemplation. The contemplation expands into the light, contacting the light with a feeling tone that is also light, in an almost physical sense.

Let the contemplation of light abide lightly, without psychological weight or property, charge or volume, until light itself is illumined, becoming translucent. Without a forced focusing, and without polarity, gravity, or fixed juxtapositions based on a subject-object relationship, this contemplation can become the body of light, a fully open channel unoccupied by a subject, by 'thingness', or by any other form of 'ness'.

This beginning contemplation has an open-ended quality. It accommodates awareness without the force of bringing energy into awareness. It has three aspects—contemplation of awareness, contemplation of relaxation, and contemplation of focused attention—and in each aspect it is fully lighter. Without the tension of awareness 'of', without paying attention, without categorizing or fixating in order to make something come alive or to accommodate interpretation, this light contemplation fuses into light and space, until light itself bonds to space. Uniquely full, not separate entities or qualities, contemplation and relaxation meet in the depth of mind and merge into one integral body, open to knowledge.

Waking Up
Through Discipline

The challenges of daily work are like a wake-up call for awareness, a reminder to use our time and energy well. Awareness in turn encourages concentration. As concentration deepens and expands, it supports discipline, and discipline creates the basis for the steady focus of sustained concentration.

Discipline is often thought of in negative terms as a harsh restraint imposed upon us by an external authority. But true discipline has a caring quality that emerges from inner knowledge. It takes form when we understand the value of our time, our energy, and the goals we have chosen to pursue. Rather than forcing us against our will, it embraces the power of willingness.

Self-discipline allows us to guide our actions along the path of the principles we most admire. It fosters the positive qualities of preparedness, order, effective and efficient action, and harmony, and gives us the power to put our vision and purpose into action. When we are disciplined, we align our image with our being, fostering integrity and deep honesty.

Through discipline, we can prepare for both the known and the unknown. Like a seasoned general, we plan for contingencies while keeping the present situation under control. If the unexpected occurs, we are ready to shift gears or change direction. As we gain experience, there are fewer events that can truly catch us by surprise: The unexpected becomes expected and is incorporated into our plans.

Maximizing Our Resources

Self-discipline allows us to maximize our inner resources. It supports a concentrated focus on present action that does not allow any distractions or interruptions. Protected by concentration from disturbances, awareness becomes sharper and more energized. When thoughts bubble up or blow across the mind like winds across a lake, awareness knows how to challenge them so they do not diminish either concentration or energy.

This strengthening awareness removes any lingering sense that discipline is restrictive or limiting. We realize that the opposite of discipline—the untrained mind—has nothing to do with real freedom and does not support lasting happiness. We see with clarity how much time and energy we have wasted in following this or that impulse, unaware of how we are using our consciousness from moment to moment. Observing how quickly a wandering mind cuts our intention, we naturally discipline ourselves to stay with our focus and put our attention and energy to work in productive ways.

Disciplined awareness supports careful planning and organization. We can articulate our goals and develop alternative strategies to achieve each goal. As events unfold, we know which path to take, and we have the flexibility and clarity to organize time, space, and knowledge accordingly.

Disciplined concentration lets us follow the plan we have decided upon, remaining steadily with each task until it is complete. This focus gives us greater control over our energy and supports the natural momentum of work. Our time and energy no longer disappear in the gaps between tasks and our work is not constantly interrupted. When we have the discipline not to break the flow of what we are doing, awareness, concentration, and energy build naturally. Fully involved, we experience a deep enjoyment. We can react instantly to new developments, making adjustments as we proceed.

Disciplined energy supports follow-through. Strong and steady, it balances body and mind, counteracting impulsive and careless action and chaotic activity. Its stability lets us act on our purpose and complete what needs to be done.

Exercise 33   Sharpening Focus

To see areas that need more discipline, look closely at the effectiveness, efficiency, and quality of your work. For example, how many times during the day do you have to go in search of something? How often do you forget where you were headed? Do you change your plan halfway through the day? How reliable is the quality of your work? How often do emergencies halt your progress? Practice asking these questions in a neutral way. The point is not to assign blame, but to pinpoint areas of difficulty where a sharper focus is needed.

Through the patience that self-discipline fosters, we grow more skilled in concentration. We can use the knowledge mined from sustained attention to make wiser decisions, for systematic planning and analysis become a natural feature of our thinking. Awareness of progress carries with it knowledge of how to make further improvements. We develop a relaxed and awakened intelligence that can readily gather resources and information, design improvements and apply them to the work at hand, and accomplish results.

Once we take up discipline willingly, we discover that we are more light and joyful in whatever we do. Even a small amount of discipline brings a clear, orderly feeling and a fresh, unburdened quality to the day. Savoring this freshness increases our delight in discipline and lays the groundwork for success.

Exercise 34   Strengthening Concentration

Notice how you cut the momentum of work in small ways: the extra trip to the coffee machine, the twenty seconds spent staring out the window. These small breaks in concentration may seem inconsequential, but they undermine the quality of your work and what you can accomplish. Discipline yourself not to take such 'vacations' from awareness. How do you react?

Checkpoints for Success

One way to support disciplined work—and a specific discipline in itself—is to practice using awareness, concentration, and energy as a yardstick to measure our work and assess whether we are heading toward success or failure. The standards and measurements we apply in our work apply equally well in our personal life, and can also be used to assess the success or failure of organizations, educational systems, and even national and international policy-making.

The brief descriptions that follow may be useful as checkpoints for monitoring the qualities of awareness, concentration, and energy in your experience. Where negative elements come to the fore, this is an indication that you need to direct your efforts there.

Awareness

When awareness is missing, time slips away and we cannot do the job. We lack the intelligence to assess what works and what does not, and we do not know how to go about training or exercising the mind. We realize that some essential knowledge is not available, but we feel too unsure of ourselves to take any action. We put off what needs to be done or else put it out of our mind, giving ourselves over to daydreams and fantasies until eventually we grow used to living our lives out of focus.

Awareness

These qualities correlate with awareness:

Positive Attentive, mindful, considerate, alert, respectful, diligent, caring, interested, enthusiastic, careful, thorough, precise, rigorous, subtle, sensitive, bright, keen, sharp, vigilant, masterful, intelligent, appreciative, receptive, delicate

Negative Thoughtless, inconsiderate, bored, mindless, indifferent, careless, numb, dull, shallow, unobservant, oblivious, distracted, negligent, ignoring, confused, daydreaming, neglectful, insensitive

---

Concentration

When we are unable to concentrate, we cannot focus on the specifics of what needs to be done, and eventually become confused about our goals and the objectives of our actions. Once we grow accustomed to being ineffective, we tell ourselves that we are not competent to do more, or devote our energy to enumerating and explaining the obstacles that prevent us from being more successful. One way or another we discourage ourselves from taking decisive action.

Energy

Without energy, our efforts are slow, sporadic, and inconsistent, and we are sharply restricted in what we can accomplish. In this society, the impor-

---

Concentration

These qualities correlate with concentration:

Positive Devoted, involved, studious, engaged, contemplative, thorough, focused, intent, steadfast, loyal, resolute, persistent

Negative Wandering, restless, unfocused, dazed, bewildered, lost, chaotic, indecisive, unstable, tentative

---

tance of energy for accomplishment has long been disguised by the role of technology, which makes available energy of a different kind. But the dream that technology could supply us with endless energy is coming to an end; we see now that energy that is not married to intelligence and awareness will produce damaging and unforeseen consequences. One of the great challenges facing us in the coming decades will be whether we can learn to cultivate the resource of human energy and direct it toward positive ends.

Investigating Interplay

At a deeper level, awareness, concentration, and energy are inseparable. For example, although concentration is linked more to the mental realm and energy more to the physical realm, mind and body each have their own forms of awareness, concentration, and energy.

> ## Energy
>
> These qualities correlate with energy:
>
> *Positive* Active, lively, vigorous, diligent, enterprising, dynamic, powerful, effective, intense, enthusiastic, spirited, encouraging, inspiring, refreshing, warm
>
> *Negative* Idle, dull, lazy, weary, bored, weak, powerless, futile, ineffective, helpless, inept, nonproductive, discouraged, intimidated

At times the interplay among these three resources can become unbalanced in quite specific ways. If awareness does not choose a goal toward which energy can be directed, energy becomes inconsistent, chaotic, and confused, and eventually turns toward dullness. Energy without concentration is scattered and restless: Instead of being productive, it feeds on dissatisfaction and tends toward extremes of emotionality and ultimately collapse. Without energy, awareness and concentration are quickly depleted; if they do continue to operate, we fall into daydreams or pleasant but essentially meaningless images.

When we become familiar with this kind of interplay, we can discover one factor operating within the others. For example, when we are highly concentrated without any real awareness, we may eventually discover within this concentration the awareness

of not being aware. To restore balance, we can activate different kinds of awareness: of mental opera-
tions, actions and their consequences, of physical
sensations, and so on. By cultivating this equality of
awareness we stimulate the energy that can awaken
concentration.

It is possible to identify imbalances in the interplay of awareness, concentration, and energy in individuals, in a single project at work, and in the rise
and fall of corporations; perhaps we can even see
such imbalances at work in the fortunes of whole
nations and civilizations. The more we look in these
ways, the more we realize that the interplay of these
three resources helps shape our human destinies.

Exercise 35 Circle of the Senses

A. Here is an exercise to balance awareness. Sitting in a relaxed way, let awareness go to each of the
senses in turn. Gradually develop a rhythm in which
awareness circulates through the senses, and make
that rhythm faster. Over the course of several minutes, take the speed of this circulation just to the
point of discomfort. See if you can relax into this
discomfort and open more fully to each sense in turn,
letting the energy of this dynamic build toward
greater awareness.

B. To expand the previous exercise, bring the
same awareness to the breath and then to the physical sensation in and behind the eyes, and add these
two elements into the circle of the senses. Be aware

of the momentum of the circulation as a separate element in the cycle as well.

C. Look for this same dynamic in other areas of experience; for instance, in times of spontaneous laughter, while you are thinking creatively, or while you are imagining new possibilities for achievement. Cultivate your sensitivity and allow it to energize every part of your experience.

Deepening Awareness, Concentration, and Energy

The interplay of awareness, concentration, and energy can also be investigated at more subtle levels. For example, it is possible to discover within energy a deeper, contemplative quality, like a stillness in the midst of motion. This quality has a meditative, calming effect that settles awareness, encourages innovative knowledge, and makes available the full light of the senses. It contributes to the panoramic aspect of awareness, giving the activity of the mind a kind of background glow, a non-specific 'seeingness' that has the quality of sharpness in the foreground and alertness in the background. In terms of the body, this 'seeingful' energy manifests as a light awareness that interacts with the body and the senses, penetrating even to the level of the cells.

It is possible to stimulate energy in such a way that we settle into its stillness, opening into the body level of awareness and letting that awareness carry us into concentration. Within this concentration, there is a sense that it is possible to open the cells of the body to knowledge and higher degrees of awareness.

Exercise 36   Observing ACE

A good beginning practice for tracing awareness, concentration and energy in operation is to take notes every day on how these factors show up in your experience. Note the effect of the weather, your working conditions, the specific demands of the job you are currently doing, your physical and mental condition, your diet, your emotions, what you sense and experience, your situation at home, and so on.

Observe those around you as well, looking for patterns. For example, young people readily manifest energy, those in their middle years are more likely to be focused and concentrated, and those who are older are more able to awaken awareness.

Another factor to evaluate is how the kind of work being done affects and draws on awareness, concentration, and energy. In some kinds of work the failure to develop certain kinds of concentration can actually be dangerous; in others a different quality of concentration, more akin to awareness, must operate if there are to be any worthwhile results. Artists and musicians need an awareness linked to sensitivity, while a successful stockbroker needs the kind of awareness that focuses on details and broad-scale trends alike, successfully balancing both. It might also be possible to discover different patterns within different ethnic or cultural groups.

Exercise 37   Chart of Self-Discovery

This practice makes use of awareness, concentration, and energy as a yardstick to assess how you are working and how you could improve your discipline. The basic exercise is to chart the rise and fall of each factor throughout the day.

The chart on the following page can be used to record your measurements. Photocopy thirty copies at an enlarged size and use them to track awareness, concentration, and energy for a month, assigning each factor a value between one (the lowest) and ten (the highest). By tracking yourself regularly you will begin to see more clearly how variations are connected both to the nature of the work and to the level of accomplishment and satisfaction. Making entries three times a day is recommended: in the early morning, at midday, and at the end of the afternoon. If you wish, you could add a fourth checkpoint in the late evening. At each checkpoint, be alert for negative judgments or feelings of guilt that discourage further efforts. Cultivate a light and pleasurable involvement that supports interest in the measurement process. In this way you will protect your focus on the work, encouraging awareness to fully engage the flow of concentration.

In addition to charting each factor separately, note their interplay. A rule of thumb for spotting imbalances is that the factor operating at the lowest level needs to be functioning at least half as effectively as the highest factor. For example, if concentration is at 8, energy and awareness must be at 4 or

Date:

Notes:

Checkpoint				
Concentration				
Awareness				
Energy				
Productivity				
Satisfaction				

10
9
8
7
6
5
4
3
2
1

Checkpoint (Time of Day)

If you wish, use the space at the left
to graph the flow of each factor.
Colored pencils are recommended.

higher; otherwise, distortions will arise, and the factor operating at higher levels will begin to deteriorate.

In this interplay, concentration should be considered the central factor. Thus, if you average the three factors, the average should be weighted toward concentration. Try a ratio of 2:1:1 to start with, and see whether this conforms to your experience. Here is another rule of thumb: a weighted average between 5 and 7 should produce good results. An average of 9 or 10 would be close to what in the Buddhist tradition is called samadhi.

In assigning numerical values to the quality of awareness, concentration, and energy in operation, you will have to develop your own standards for measurement, for at present we lack the shared experience that would allow us to develop a more objective approach. In any case, it is your own experience and your own patterns that count. By conducting this kind of detailed inquiry, you will develop data and knowledge concerning your own capabilities and patterns, learn how to develop your own resources more fully, and prepare yourself to take on bigger challenges and opportunities.

Beyond the levels described here, awareness, concentration, and energy could each be said to operate at a level that we cannot ordinarily touch in our work. Although that is a topic for another time, the focus being recommended here is a good preparation for further inquiry.

Communication

Working well with others depends on good communication. Before we can communicate clearly with others, however, we need to be able to communicate well with ourselves. Communication is more than simply passing information from one person to another through spoken or written messages; it is also a matter of emotions, attitudes, and intentions communicated through our tone of voice, gestures, actions, and decisions. If we ignore this larger context, our efforts to communicate are likely to be unsuccessful.

Behind good communication is a caring quality based on honesty and sensitivity. Without this caring, our attempts to communicate are often obstructed by subtle negative emotions that disrupt our sensitivity and awareness. In the grip of these emotions, we find it difficult to hear others accurately and are unlikely to be heard ourselves. For instance, while we may think we are communicating something necessary and thus positive, we may actually be passing on our impatience, anger, anxiety, dislike, or desire. If our emotions are strong, we may end up blaming the other party for the resulting breakdown in communication.

A panoramic awareness of our own states of mind gives us the clarity we need to improve our communication. We can learn to pay attention in a neutral way, observing which of our actions and moods undermine our attempts to communicate, and take steps to prevent this from happening. By refining awareness and developing sensitivity and thoughtfulness, we can learn to respond perceptively to the subtle inner rhythms that govern our own emotions and thought processes and more easily tune in to others as well.

Clarity is the door to good communication, and patience is its key. With patience we hear more deeply, understanding the significance of the communication rather than just the words. We see more fully, not ignoring or avoiding. We can watch to see if others truly understand what we wish to communicate; we can try several ways to say something and use imagery to facilitate understanding. We can ask others to 'play back' what we have said to confirm that the communication has been clear. As we learn to relate to each individual in a positive and truly effective way, communication becomes a process of sharing, of opening to knowledge.

When communication aims at accomplishment rather than self-protection, our ability to communicate effectively improves dramatically. Our responses come easily and dynamically, and are brief, clear, and concise. We are able to cut through excessive talk and penetrate to the heart of the matter at hand. Our rough edges become smoother; our patience and good will strengthen. Whatever the content of what we have to say, we are able to express an inspiring and motivating quality that helps everyone to direct energy toward what needs to be accomplished. We speak in ways that invite participation and encourage each individual to build on his or her strengths and positive qualities. We learn how to accommodate each person's way of approaching work, helping to make work truly valuable for others. Through our good influence we establish mutual trust and shared understanding.

Communicating about Problems

As our skill grows, we can also learn to communicate more openly about problems. Many of us have learned from painful experience the difficulty of communicating anything negative. Beneath all the reasons we give for not speaking out lies fear: We want to avoid confrontation or emotionality, prevent others from pointing out our own flaws, or keep hidden the many things that we would rather not see.

Refusing to confront an existing problem may seem like a realistic response. Perhaps it is not 'our' problem at all. And if we see no solution, why bring it up? But this view is short-sighted, for if we stand by and ignore a problem that could harm others, we too are causing harm, and we too will suffer.

By ignoring a problem, we are agreeing to a conspiracy of silence. Refusing to challenge this realm of willful ignorance gives not-knowing the power to threaten our creative work and our goals. It cheats everyone out of knowledge, and causes great damage to the community within which we work.

Instead of avoiding confrontation in difficult situations, we can learn to speak 'through' our fear of confrontation and be more honest with one another. Even though we may start with no solutions to offer, listening and questioning may uncover new perspectives and possibilities. Acknowledging the negative side of a situation and seeing the mistakes and failures that have been made is a necessary step, but the negative side does not need to be proclaimed again and again. We can use a positive approach, encouraging ourselves and others to learn from mistakes and looking for successes and positive potential.

By bringing difficulties out into the open before they become serious problems, we increase the likelihood that we can find solutions in a timely way. Dealing with problems early on can save much pain and suffering, time and energy. Once we develop greater honesty, we discover that we can afford to trust one another, and that open communication gets better results than hiding.

When co-workers share a way of working based on caring and responsibility, they can function positively and dynamically together. This working style creates strong individuals willing to dedicate themselves to meaningful work. It cuts through the superficial camaraderie that substitutes for real caring and thus undermines accomplishment. When we communicate through words and actions that are true to our own values and goals, we exert a consistently positive influence on others and move naturally toward achieving our goals.

Exercise 38   Opening Communication

We all know someone we have difficulty communicating with. Next time you must interact with such a person, practice awareness. Speak with care and listen well, not taking things personally. Set fighting, disagreement, and emotional reactions aside, and be diplomatic, avoiding confrontation. Afterward, take the time to record your observations in your journal.

Exercise 39   Group Discussion

What problems within your work group are you aware of that you cannot bring out into the open? Speak to a few of your colleagues to see if they perceive the same need for changes or discussion. Does a momentum build for meeting to discuss the issue? Remember that problems are always easier to discuss earlier rather than later.

Exercise 40   Relationships

Pick someone with whom you have a good working relationship and resolve to do all you can to support that person—sharing problems, making suggestions, and keeping communication open and clear. One way to strengthen your shared understanding is by practicing communication that does not depend on words.

Exercise 41 Visualizing Communication

A. When something is not going well at work, let yourself imagine the problem and everyone involved in it. Now imagine yourself expressing your view of the situation to them in a full and complete way. Do not hesitate to bring into play your sense of humor and your sense of the meaning and fullness of life. Let the scene play out to the point where understanding arises and the problem dissolves.

B. At the start of your work day, imagine that the other people you are working with are your friends, that you share the same goals and purposes, and that you will work together easily and lightly, offering one another support and good communication. As you begin to work, hold this image and its associated thoughts steady. Renew the practice during the day.

Do this daily for two weeks. This confident, friendly approach attracts support: People recognize that you have something positive to offer and welcome working with you. Whatever its sources, resistance tends to melt away.

Exercise 42 Throat Energy

The dynamic energy of the throat combines the power of the voice with the power of words. Whenever you speak at work, stay in touch with the energy of the throat. Start by relaxing the throat and the belly, and practice listening to the sound of your voice and the qualities you are communicating at a level beneath content. You can refine your ability to do this by uniting awareness of sound with the breath. When the energy of the throat is balanced and flowing smoothly, you will find you can express yourself well, with great effect on others.

Cultivate an even and pleasant way of speaking, without regard to your emotional reactions. With practice, you will find that the sound of the words brings vivid feedback that allows you to adjust the flow of energy in the throat. For further suggestions on how to open and relax the throat, see Exercise 46, p. 150, Exercise C, p. 248, and *Kum Nye Relaxation*, Part 1, pp. 35–54.

Sharing Knowledge

Respect for those we work with and honesty in our dealings with others finds its natural expression in a sense of teamwork. Out of the wish to help others accomplish their own goals and a shared vision of what we can do together, we naturally see through the typical possessive and competitive attitudes that cause so much frustration in our work. We move toward a way of working in which we share what we know with others, aware that in this way we make our knowledge more effective and prepare for success at a higher level.

Human civilization is based on the sharing of knowledge, yet in our work relationships we tend to hoard the special knowledge we have. We are often advised to think of such unique knowledge as the key to our success: the one factor that singles us out from everyone else. From this perspective, it would be foolish to share our knowledge. We would risk losing our special status and might even put our livelihood in jeopardy.

However, this self-centered way of working and thinking is bound to undermine our efforts to make use of work as a means for developing our inner resources. What is more, if we can count on a spirit of teamwork within our organization or work group, cooperative effort is sure to be more effective in achieving the shared goals of the group.

Once a basis for trust and communication is operating, we recognize that our willingness to share the knowledge we have is what makes us a truly valuable member of the organization or team we work with. Sharing knowledge allows us to contribute to the welfare of the whole. It also cuts through the short-range, small-minded thinking that plagues our own efforts at realization.

If we have accumulated special knowledge, our long-range goal should be to share it so completely that our co-workers no longer need to rely on us. In this way everyone is free to move forward, and we ourselves can constantly be exploring new fields of accomplishment and inquiry. When the members of a work group or a company share this attitude, they will automatically do their best to ensure the success of the whole operation.

When each person is committed to sharing what he or she knows, awareness, concentration, and energy flow throughout the organization in the same way that blood circulates through the body. As members of an organization or team learn how different aspects of the work fit together, the group as a whole can make better use of its time and energy. A firm basis for accomplishment develops, and problems

that might have seemed overwhelming before become readily manageable.

For each of us as individuals, sharing what we
know helps us develop a deeper view: an appreciation for knowledge wherever it manifests. We see
more clearly how our work connects to that of others.
As our vision widens, we learn to care for one another
and to take responsibility without regard to titles, job
descriptions, and past history. This does not mean
interfering with others or involving ourselves where
there is no need to do so. But it does mean being
ready to help and to contribute.

Sharing in this way transcends the likes and dis-
likes, manipulative or self-centered friendships, and
partiality that dominate so many of our relationships, in work as in the rest of our lives. The focus
on accomplishment can be a powerful catalyst for
dissolving these self-defeating approaches. Confident that we are all working together for shared ends,
we learn to respect one another, for we realize that
each person contributes to the whole. Seeing the
strengths and weaknesses of each of our co-workers,
we become more even-handed and neutral, capable
of acting in the best interests of all concerned. Preju-
dice and personal bias give way to tolerance and
support. We acknowledge that each person has his
or her own space, authority, knowledge, values, and
judgments, and even where we disagree there is
room for cooperation. Expanding from this mutual
respect, the intention to share what we know develops toward an all-encompassing morality.

Ways of Sharing

Once we have resolved to set aside oneupsmanship and destructive competition, we can share knowledge in friendly ways, sensitive to whether what we know really needs to be communicated and whether it will find a receptive audience. What we have to offer may be specific techniques, past experience, insights, or knowledge relating to work itself. In any situation, we can present what we know in a light, inspiring way. Simple and sometimes humorous examples can often help bring clarity and deepen everyone's enjoyment.

Whenever we discover useful knowledge, we can look for appropriate ways and times to pass it on; whenever we develop new skills worth sharing, we can let others know. Together, we can take pleasure in helping one another mine our collective knowledge and develop our inner resources. This kind of sharing is the mark of real friendship. In one way or another, we can extend it to everyone we work with.

An important element in sharing knowledge is offering genuine appreciation for the contributions made by others. In this way we demonstrate that we care about the work we are doing and the people we work with. Our care and appreciation cheer everyone's spirits and build relationships on a basis of strength and commitment.

As we come to rely on one another to share the knowledge we have, we can all work together efficiently, without duplicating effort or wasting time. We can plan well, following through and following up, checking with others to see whether they have carried out their specific responsibilities. We can demonstrate for each other how to relax and refresh the senses and how to appreciate the details of work. When difficulties arise, we can turn away from blame toward the knowledge that will let us deal with the situation most effectively, giving one another the strong support that is the best guarantee of results.

It is especially important to share these attitudes and specific ways of working with newcomers. On the one hand, someone new to the organization needs to master skills that we already know; on the other hand, the new worker is looking for clues as to how others relate to their work and what opportunities the work offers. If we pass on the value of enjoying our time and being productive, we can help each new worker and support the organization at the same time. We can also learn from each new individual, drawing on her or his experience and integrating it into the understanding of the whole group.

Beyond specific skills and information, the most valuable knowledge we can share is the knowledge of how to use our inner resources—awareness, concentration, and energy—to develop knowledge, discipline, and responsibility. By passing on this understanding, we give others the opportunity and ability to learn for themselves. Transmitting whatever we learn about ways to challenge our limits and expand our abilities, through words or by example, we bring this knowledge to fruition and help create the path to success for others and for ourselves.

Exercise 43   Responsibility for Knowledge

A. Notice how well someone around you is working and think about how you could contribute to that person's work. Perhaps just a word of encouragement or appreciation could make a difference. Act on what you decide and observe the results.

B. Each day plan to learn something new in some area of your work. Do not hesitate to ask someone to share his or her knowledge, but be careful not to infringe on that person's work time or energy.

C. What do you know that you have not put to use? How are you hoarding knowledge? Can you activate more knowledge today?

Exercise 44   Sharing Deeper Knowledge

Starting today, find ways to share with someone one of the key points you have learned about developing awareness, concentration, and energy. This may be by example rather than words, or by the kind of work you assign that person or the kind of feedback you give. What is the most valuable knowledge you have discovered? How can you make it available to someone else in a effective way?

PART THREE

Transforming Work

Lightening Energy

Awareness, concentration, and energy can be a yardstick to measure our progress and a mirror to help us see how we are working. If we encourage ourselves to be aware and mindful in dealing with daily detail, we will soon notice significant progress in our productivity, the quality of our work experience, and our sense of well-being. As we accomplish more, awareness increases, activating knowledge that we can use to transform the confusion, emotionality, and habitual responses that cut our energy and undermine the quality of our experience.

The mind constantly responds to sense impressions received by the body and interprets and labels physical feelings. When this interrelationship between body and mind is not balanced, mental and physical energies do not flow smoothly and evenly, and tension builds up. As a result, energy is diverted into internal dialogues, excuses, and emotional reactions such as fear, guilt, hostility, lack of confidence, and defensiveness.

Awareness has the power to free the energy presently locked within these negative patterns. It shows us how mind and body are interacting, and gives us the opportunity to take action to change. Applying awareness in this way opens a new level of achievement and well-being. It is no longer just a question of using our resources with maximum effectiveness, but of transforming their operation. Success at this level gives work a whole new dimension of meaning.

To awaken the awareness we need to bring about this change, we can practice balancing the flow of energy in the body and through the senses. Balanced energy enriches sense experience and makes awareness lighter and clearer. We can then put this lightness and clarity to use in observing our experience, generating the knowledge that can direct our energies in fruitful ways.

Disconnections

From childhood on, the smooth flow and harmonious integration of our energies are undermined by a fundamental sense of isolation and confusion so basic that it may even trace to a time before birth. Trapped in this isolation, the mind operates in its own space, circulating a network of thoughts and ideas, images and memories. The senses and feelings function in another, disconnected space.

These disconnections have far-reaching consequences. Unable to communicate with the head, the heart withdraws and falls silent; when it does speak, the head cannot make sense of what is being said. Gradually we stop caring about what is happening to us. The vital energy of the belly is cut off from both

146

the heart and the head, and so there is no flowing, dynamic force in our actions and thoughts.

Throughout childhood and into our adult lives, we seek out experiences that restore the sense of a more integrated way of being. But because we do not really understand what is happening, we achieve this sense of wholeness only rarely. With no grounded power behind awareness, our energy is undirected and tends to become caught up in memories and images, habitual attitudes, bodily stances, and emotional moods. We learn to recycle energy into emotionality, reinforcing and restimulating agitation and irritation, dullness and depression. Since concentration has no dependable fuel, thoughts fragment and move incoherently. Enthusiasm and motivation decline. We lose confidence in ourselves and begin a downward spiral into failure and regret. Our natural sense of stability and our integrity and responsiveness fade away.

Connecting and Integrating

Although these patterns are in one sense firmly established, we can learn to counteract them. Through awareness of the senses, we can increase the flow of energy through the body centers and enrich the quality of sense experience. We can connect the energy of the heart to both the belly and the head and heal the isolation and yearning we feel. Once these new connections have been made, gut-level will power can circulate through the heart, strengthening and supporting it. Thoughts can flow smoothly and effectively, growing reliable and clear, and real vision can emerge to guide our lives. We are not so apt to be overwhelmed when experience becomes confusing, and we will not fall so easily into emotional reactions. When the heart is strong and the will stands firmly behind it, we do not quit or panic, lash out against others, or withdraw in the face of obstacles.

As body and mind become more integrated and coordinated, our 'normal' energy level increases. We can readily give more energy to our work without pressuring or forcing ourselves. Our way of working becomes more dynamic and creative, feeding back positive results and genuine satisfaction that encourage us to increase awareness, concentration, and energy still further.

Lighter Awareness

As the energy flow through the body centers increases, enriching the quality of sense experience, awareness becomes lighter. The more the energy of the head center lightens and the chest opens, the lighter awareness becomes. This light mind energy becomes a catalyst for action, lightening negative patterns and activating new knowledge. It brings with it a cheerful, positive quality that allows us to manifest the spirit, charisma, and character that bring success.

We can discover this panoramic light awareness encircling each thought, like the diffused halo of light surrounding a candle flame. Gently opening and unfolding, it illuminates the functioning of the senses, the movement of perception, all aspects of thinking, and even the physiological functions of the body. We can see more clearly how emotional responses block the openness and flow of energy and can draw on awareness to lighten the effect of such responses on body and mind.

As energy flows more freely through all parts of the body, we can invite rich flavors into sense experience and expand them into deeply satisfying and fulfilling sensations. This cherishing, healing quality refines the translucent energy surrounding thought, making awareness lighter and experience ever richer and deeper. We are full of vitality, and natural intelligence operates freely.

The light energy of awareness relieves the pressure of thoughts and fears, emotions, excuses, and internal dialogues. Awareness receives each thought with full responsibility, lightening what is heavy and melting what is frozen. Opening to its light, we see with the eyes of a master, enjoying the light-show of thoughts and feelings like playful images on a screen.

Exercise 45   Reversing the Patterning

One of the most effective ways to generate a freer flow of energy is through relaxation. Exercise B on p. 247 provides a simple introduction to relaxation; Exercise P on p. 256 deepens this approach, and other exercises are given below. Many other practices that focus on relaxation through breathing, movement, and self-massage can be found in *Kum*

Nye Relaxation, Parts 1 and 2 (Berkeley: Dharma Publishing, 1978).

Exercise 46 Inviting Openness

This exercise is for individuals who are comfortable with a more contemplative approach to awareness and energy. The purpose is to lighten and open the energy centers of the body by focusing on each one in turn.

Begin with the throat. Set aside half an hour each day, morning or evening, to sit quietly and concentrate lightly on the throat. Breathe gently through both nose and mouth, with the mouth slightly open and the tip of the tongue lightly touching the upper palate just behind the front teeth. Breathing in this way may be awkward at first, but with a little practice, you will feel its beneficial effects, which come from balancing the energy of the throat and distributing energy more evenly to the head and heart. Relax into this way of breathing, without worrying about doing it correctly; the quality of the breath will soon become open and natural.

Let this gentle breath calm and settle the throat. Allow your awareness to merge lightly with the breath. Once you notice a feeling of relaxation anywhere in the body, deepen and enjoy it by joining the breath and awareness to it. After the second day, lighten the quality of your concentration so that body energy can flow more freely.

After you have concentrated on the throat center for three days, move the focus to the head, concentrating on a spot between the eyes. Then move the focus to the heart center and finally to the belly. Grow familiar with the different qualities of these energy centers. The energy that is released will invite steadier concentration and more vivid awareness.

Exercise 47   Light Centers

Sitting quietly, visualize light in the center of energy between the eyes. Then move to the throat, the heart, and the belly, taking a few minutes for each center. Let the light be very intense, like sunlight reflecting off snow.

Exercise 48   Sensing Space

Imagine a spacious quality active throughout the body. Bring this spaciousness to each of the body centers in turn, beginning with the head. This light spaciousness expands and loosens the space of each body center, and gently begins to release any blocked energy. When a flowing sensation arises, sensitively join awareness and concentration with it. You may experience a new sense of intelligence, stability, and vitality, reflecting this integration of awareness, concentration, and energy.

Exercise 49   Relaxing the Senses

Energy often becomes constricted in the head because we focus our senses so tightly. Usually our eyes look straight ahead, like horses with blinders on. Similarly, we listen narrowly, focusing on sounds 'in our heads'. The following practices counter this tightness and can be done anytime while working. They are especially useful if your job involves computer or phone work.

A. Several times each day, relax your eyes and move them lightly from side to side and up and down. Let the head remain still. As you do this, relax the effort to focus the eyes, so that the movement has a smooth, sweeping quality. This motion stimulates awareness and opens up a broader, more flexible view.

B. As you work, try listening to sounds as though they were happening miles away. What is the effect on your awareness? On your concentration?

Seeing through Reasons and Excuses

Once we have stimulated new energy and activated a lighter awareness, we can use these resources to question our self-imposed limitations and open up higher dimensions of accomplishment. Work is our testing ground, the arena where we can see clearly the results of applying our knowledge. Here we have a chance to see in action the habitual patterns that hold us back from creative action. For example, how do we react when we are truly challenged in our work? How do we respond to small demands that interrupt our routine?

River of Excuses

Even if we are strongly motivated to do well in our work, certain kinds of challenges trigger an almost automatic response: reasons and excuses for not responding. Carried along by its own momentum, a current of reasonable excuses runs through consciousness like a subterranean river. It winds its way into thoughts and images, its murmur so familiar we hardly notice it. Taking form in words, it delivers messages and tells stories so normal and acceptable there is nothing to make us pay special attention: "I can't do that." "I'm not sure." "I don't know how." "I don't want to." "I'll do it later." "I'll try." We trade such messages back and forth almost without thinking, until they become unquestionable.

Counseling us to put things off, to ignore challenges, to take no risks, the current of excuses lulls awareness into an uneasy sleep. Did we intend to write a letter? Make a phone call or meet a schedule or commitment? Weaving a thick fabric of dreams, reasons, and explanations and wrapping it around us, the mind tells us it is all right to let go of our concerns and postpone our commitments. We can take care of them later—or perhaps if we dismiss them, they will eventually disappear entirely. Alternatively, the mind may trigger an endless string of worries and feelings of guilt—excuses at a different level that keep us so occupied we cannot concentrate on simply doing the job.

The familiar rhythm and momentum of excuses protect us from any unaccustomed situations. When a challenge arises and a decision must be made, we may hardly notice. Absorbed in listening to the old tune, we can slide so quickly off the point of decision into an excuse that we are scarcely aware our inaction has made the decision for us.

At some level, we know that time is being wasted and opportunities are passing away. The body is a more truthful witness than our thoughts: We may sometimes experience a sickening sensation in the gut or a draining feeling in the chest; we may get headaches or sense a thick fogginess between the eyes or suddenly feel sleepy. But these sensations are so commonplace we endure them without question.

Over time, this way of thinking and acting corrodes our initial commitment and enthusiasm. As the years go by, we may wonder why our energy and confidence seem to be decreasing and our efforts are producing fewer results than we had hoped. Is it just that we are growing older?

Self-Justifying Excuses

Whatever the content of the excuses we give, the flavor of what is said is so reasonable that we naturally accept it as true. Often we may not even realize that we are giving an excuse. It was not our fault: We fell ill, we never really agreed, something urgent came up. Our feelings, our emotions, even our body language quickly fall into line.

Most people learn early on how to make reasonable excuses, and the smartest people are the most highly skilled. "I'm sorry," we say, asking for our shortcomings to be forgiven and expecting that they will be. Yet every successful excuse marks a lost opportunity. Now that everything is 'all right', there is no impetus to challenge the patterns that led to failure in the first place or to learn from our mistakes.

We tend to use excuses to 'make more room' in our lives. But this is a superficial view. Although we may seem to buy time by making an excuse, there is no 'extra' time to be bought, and the time spent making excuses and convincing ourselves to believe them has been spoiled for positive accomplishment. But that is not all. Each time we make an excuse, we strengthen our own sense of limits. As we rub backs with the part of mind that supports our limitations, we soon succeed in crippling our own abilities and discouraging others as well. Even our casual farewells—"Have fun! And don't work too hard!"—are actually a subtle form of undermining.

Excuses demonstrate convincingly that there is nothing more we can do. They leave us unable to open the doors to positive sources of inspiration. We miss opportunities to awaken awareness because we are not even looking for them. Chances to develop encouragement, discipline, and confidence pass us by. Simple positive messages—"I could do that!"—elude us because our energy is bonded to a negative view. Refusing to acknowledge the difference it would make if we responded positively to challenges and opportunities, we hide our best qualities behind a screen of words and emotions. We actually present our limitations as our chosen way to be.

Not Wanting to be Responsible

Sometimes when we observe other people caught up in their excuses, we may dislike what we see. But still we continue to act the same way ourselves. We may even use their weakness to justify our own. No one else is taking risks or taking responsibility—why should we be any different? Ironically, we use our intelligence to hold on to weakness, treating our weakness as if it were our greatest strength.

In the back of our minds, we may feel deeply disappointed at this failure to exercise our abilities. Still, unless we make a strong commitment to awareness, we will continue to cover up the truth of what is going on with emotional reactions that feed another layer of excuses. We feel too embarrassed or too sick at heart, too guilty or too ashamed to acknowledge that we are our own private self-deceiver. Ambivalent and unhappy, knowing that we are not making the best use of our time and life, we sacrifice our own vision and inspiration.

Recklessly mind spins out reasons and emotions, adding to the web of excuses. Because we know at some level what we are doing, our imagination may become inflamed with worry about the mess we are creating and panicked at the thought of having to fix it. Physical reactions flare up and multiply. Problems—including illness or accidents—pop up in all directions, manifesting our wish not to wake up, not to be responsible.

If we are willing to bring more awareness to the excuse-making process, we soon see that excuses strengthen a sense of hopelessness, shortage, and limitation. Supporting our highest values, awareness wakes us up to a healthier and more balanced way of using the precious time available to us.

Exercise 50   Penetrating Reasons

A. Notice the reasons you give whenever you do not keep an agreement or a promise. Listen particularly for statements that begin with I: "I couldn't get

157

anyone to help." "I never said . . . ." "I didn't have time." Also look for explanations that focus on factors beyond your control: "He was on vacation." "The computer crashed." "I didn't have the right tool." Remember that the reasons you give will sound completely convincing to yourself and probably to others. What kind of shift is necessary before you can see them as excuses?

B. Once you start to recognize excuses in what previously seemed like good reasons, start a master list of excuses. Look for repetitions and variations.

Exercise 51   Stopping Excuses

A. Whenever you give a reason for not doing something at work, ask: "Is this an excuse or not?" If you catch yourself making an excuse, try just stopping, even if it means breaking off in the middle of a sentence. What are you protecting by making excuses? If you stop making as many excuses, how do those you work with react? Be prepared for their possible discomfort.

B. Here is a more radical version of the same exercise. For a whole day, whenever somebody asks you to do something at work, just say yes, and do it!

Recognizing
Negative Patterns

When we first begin a new job or project, a sense of possibilities unfolds before us. Interested and starting fresh, we feel responsive and energetic, and our awareness and commitment are high. Gradually, however, enthusiasm fades; six months later we are taking the work for granted. Awareness dims, concentration weakens, and energy is absorbed in emotional patterns. Our ability to accomplish something of value drops dramatically. Others may be satisfied with the work we are doing, but compared to our full potential, we are almost at a standstill. From an open field of possibilities, we have drifted into the familiar world of limitation.

When our awareness is low, we do not recognize how this shift comes about. Not sensitive to the internal dialogues and emotional patterns that undermine our ability, we allow mind to manipulate us into choosing against our own best interests. We end up wasting our time in playing negative roles that discourage and limit us.

All of us know that we fall into playing certain negative roles, but we may shy away from investigating them; if challenged, we may even defend them. The path of awareness calls for a different approach. It shows us that recognizing our weaknesses is an essential step in marshalling our resources for success.

Contemplating Negative Roles

At the back of the mind we may sense a strong opposition to looking at negative roles. This opposition may surface in impatience or irritation, numbness or disinterest, but beneath these reactions is fear that the experience will be painful. When we protect the field of resistance, we are simply prolonging the fear of pain, oblivious to the pain that comes through fear itself.

The practice of concentration gives us an alternative. Quietly concentrating on a role we have been playing allows us to defuse the emotions and thoughts gathered within it. If we can concentrate fully on a negative role for even a few minutes, mind can catch up to mind: Embracing memory in the present moment, mind can see its nature. The sharp sword of painful memories loses its cutting edge; the role we play loses its force and may even disappear. Then we can turn the healing power of awareness and concentration to cultivating healthier responses.

Pointers to Negativity

One way to recognize the negative roles we play is by observing them as they are acted out by others. Here are some examples to look for:

The Fighter The chest is puffed out and the mouth turned down, as if the person were ready to pick a fight. A typical inner dialogue: "I work so hard and I don't get any recognition—why should I keep on trying?" When we act from this attitude, we prevent ourselves from enjoying our work and end up always feeling dissatisfied. Work goes very slowly. Awareness goes into 'spacing out', wasting time, or finding any excuse to keep from concentrating fully.

The Duchess The head is thrown back slightly, the lips are curled, and the eyes are narrowed. A typical inner dialogue: "I've already taken care of that. You don't have to remind me. I have more important things to do." When we play this role, we do our work hastily and often badly. We do not view it as a personal responsibility.

The Failure The chest is caved in and the head hangs down. A typical inner dialogue: "I already have too much to do. I couldn't possibly take on one more job." When we play this role, we feel overwhelmed and keep falling behind in our work; we may seem to be working hard, but our communication is poor, our energy scattered, and our awareness confused.

The Complainer The defining gesture is shrugging the shoulders and shaking the head. A typical inner dialogue: "I can't believe how unprofessional and disorganized these people are. This project is bound to fail." When we play this role we cannot imagine being responsible for what others are doing; we have difficulty working well in a team, and we use complaining as a way to stay connected and feel important.

The Dreamer The head is tilted up and the eyes stare into space amid many sighs. An inner dialogue: "If only things were different, I could succeed." When we act from this attitude we will not take responsibility for ourselves or our work. While we feel our abilities are underutilized, we do not take responsibility to develop them.

Once we recognize a role being played out by someone else and develop a clear understanding of its consequences, we can look to see if we play the same role. We may be able to recognize how playing these roles sets us up for failure and disappointment that trigger other typical patterns:

The Quitter When we seem to be failing no matter what we do, we fill our hearts and minds with negative fantasies. We tell ourselves that we lack the knowledge or training or resources we need; we weigh ourselves down with feelings of incompetence. These negative messages push us deeper into emotionality, depression, and inertia. It does not take long before we convince ourselves that we have no choice but to give up. We may sense there are alternatives, but we feel too unworthy to stimulate our energy in a positive direction. Our body, mind, and senses close down, so that even if positive thoughts, feelings, or energy do arise, they cannot flow freely. Our creativity is blocked, our intelligence blacks out, and we are unable to see a way out. Not daring to set goals and reach for them, we must give up our best hopes and dreams, and with them our self-respect.

The Pretender In the face of failure, we may tell ourselves that we are successful, distorting our perception or filling our minds with daydreams. "Tomorrow will be better," we say. "Later on I'll accomplish something; right now I'm still learning." "I don't understand why they're so angry at me—all things considered, I'm doing pretty well." Instead of facing our difficulties and making a wholehearted effort to move toward our goal, we invest our energy in trying to convince ourselves and others that we are doing our best against overwhelming odds. Covering up our underlying unwillingness to take responsibility with ungrounded optimism, we generate 'good ideas' and 'good energy' without ever penetrating to the real roots of a problem. Wanting to be appreciated for making an effort, we value approval more than the attainment of the goal, which we secretly gave up on long ago. But our superficial efforts only cause more delays, waste, and disappointment. Soon our 'good energy' has dissipated with little to show for it.

The True Believer When problems seem overwhelming, we can always hope for a miracle. "If I have faith," we tell ourselves, "everything will turn out all right. I just have to surrender to what is happening." This 'blind faith' lets us stop thinking about our problems and excuses our lack of responsibility: "Somehow it will turn out all right. Someone will find a way to fix everything."

163

The Agnostic There are many versions of this approach, ranging from 'hard-headed' realism to fatalistic 'spirituality'. We may say, "All goals are illusory," or "Nothing has any meaning anyway," or "It's all God's will." Whatever the flavor of our not-caring, it becomes the justification for our failure to take responsibility.

Life-Denying Patterns

Such stories and styles are so familiar and common it is difficult to see how destructive they are. Each of them renounces the heart of our human heritage: freedom, knowledge, compassion, creativity, love, and caring. Whatever the different colors and designs, the underlying fabric is the same: "Life is ultimately meaningless; there's no value to be gained and nothing worthwhile to accomplish. It's hopeless, and anyway, I can't do it."

When we take refuge in such thoughts, we are letting the mind deceive us with its destructive games. Mystifying and playing tricks on itself, the mind makes up reasons and excuses, lodges complaints, and pays lip service to our potential, all the while undermining our abilities. It tells us we are short of time, energy, materials, or knowledge; it discourages our growth and exhausts our positive attitudes. What choices do we have left? Only to complain, dream, and feel disappointed? This self-condemnation is worse than anything anyone else could do to us.

In the grip of these false refuges, we hold on to fantasies, seek out distracting pleasures, and cloak ourselves in laziness. We do not dare to explore our own potential or recognize the successful accomplishments of others. It is not difficult to predict the outcome: more failure, leading to less interest and involvement, leading to more denial and greater isolation, leading to more failure.

When life-denying stories steal our energy, they turn confidence and good intentions into doubt and confusion, and direct our resources and time away from accomplishment. In the end we grow convinced that limitation, conflict, and ultimately failure are inescapable.

Power of Realization

Awareness can cut through negativity by showing us what we are doing to ourselves. The first indication is a jolt of recognition: We see these roles in operation in our own attitudes and actions. Immediately we feel a sense of waste, as we glimpse how much time and opportunity we have lost.

To receive the full benefit of this realization, we must learn to stay with this knowledge. It is something like learning to ride a horse: The ride can be bumpy, and if we are unsure of what we are doing, we risk being thrown onto the rocky soil of denial and negativity. But once we learn to stay in the saddle and apply our intelligence, we are free to discover a special sense of joy and well-being.

When we first see how much our negativity and excuses have cost us, we may feel shocked or guilty.

Worry and anxiety may build up forcefully; we may even tell ourselves quite consciously that we cannot afford to face this truth. Just as we lie in bed for a few more minutes after we wake up in the morning, we may decide that there is no need to act just yet. Giving in to the habit of delay imprinted on our consciousness, we may put off change for now: "It's not the right time to take all this on."

Perhaps this move makes us feel we are 'off the hook', as if we have somehow outsmarted time. But there is no way to get the better of time. Time presents both cause and effect; time is the judge of what is real. We may think we measure time, but really it is time that measures us.

In the face of truth, guilt or worry are simply emotional responses that invite us to cut off the shock of what we are seeing. If we can relax such responses and stay with our new awareness, we can open our hearts and rejoice in the power of the understanding we have gained. This joy can be fully positive, heartfelt, and encouraging—a celebration that encompasses even our worst mistakes. The sense of waste is truly painful, but the pain we feel is inseparable from realization. Now we know what we have been doing, and our knowledge protects us. We will not get caught in that negativity again.

Recognizing how we have conducted ourselves in the past lays the groundwork for responsibility and transformation. Past mistakes and missed opportunities become the messengers of time, waking us up and inviting us to join in a new dynamic. Strengthening awareness, developing stronger concentration, and exercising better control over our energy, we can learn to track our negativities. We can hear them in the voice, sense them in the body, and watch them in our thoughts.

As awareness deepens our knowledge, we become convinced beyond any doubt that these negative patterns have nothing to offer us. Then we can release them and open more fully to present experience. Our ears can hear the music of this unique moment in time, our eyes can see its beauty, our knowledge can uncover its emerging meaning. With this new understanding, we can be confident in our ability to make productive use of the time available to us.

Drawing on Experience

Through the power of awareness, we can learn from each experience, no matter whether it is positive or negative. Observing carefully, we can test our understanding and resolve so that knowledge is strengthened at each step. Watching to see how we respond in each situation, we can transform old attitudes and explore different ways to use our human resources.

Once we understand how to challenge and transform old patterns, anything that happens is part of the process of learning and growing. Even emotional difficulties in our relationships or at work can become a way to see ourselves in action and review our progress. When energy is blocked, we can embrace this blockage and the energy it holds as a useful source of understanding. We can concentrate on physical discomfort or mental pain, gently sorting through their components and freeing their vital energy for productive work. We can deliberately challenge different features of experience: When we feel tired or dull, or are not very successful at something, or do not complete a job, or are impatient or displeased with others, we can explore ways to transform what is happening into a source of greater understanding.

Like a scientist combining chemicals to make a formula or an artist mixing colors on the palette, we can explore different combinations of mental events to develop our consciousness in fruitful and interesting ways. As we identify our weaknesses, we can use blends of awareness, concentration, and energy as catalysts to turn them into strengths. Disruptions in our routine can be part of our exploration; being stuck can also be part of the design. Whatever happens, we can continue to engage our responses, actions, feelings, and thoughts creatively, enriching the quality of our lives and making all of life a tapestry of beautiful designs and patterns.

By developing concentration, building up inner strength, and witnessing our progress, we can move from one level to the next, until we discover how to enjoy whatever we are doing and guide each action toward success. Our embodiment expresses enjoyment as our reality and our rationale. Challenging experience with ever-increasing skill, we make continuous progress, celebrating our successes along the way. When an unfamiliar challenge arises, we welcome it without fear, enjoying the newness of the unknown, never sidetracked by excuses, hesitation, laziness, or procrastination.

We often say that life is a journey and knowledge is like a book. Perhaps we could join these two images, saying that life is a journey through our own book of knowledge. If we read with intelligence, it does not matter how the plot unfolds: Each chapter closes with greater understanding and appreciation. In this book of knowledge that is our life, we can learn to read with great delight and joy the stories of our own success.

Exercise 52   Transforming Negativity

Pick random moments during the day to check on your physical posture. Note how the postures and gestures you adopt reflect habitual energy patterns and emotions. For instance, do you stand proudly with your hands on your hips? Cross your arms defensively over your chest? Hang your head glumly, rest your chin in your hands and stare into space? Tighten your shoulders fearfully?

When you find a typical posture, look for the attitude it manifests. What gestures and facial expressions are characteristic of the attitude? How is the attitude expressed in internal dialogue? How does the theme of the internal dialogue arise in disguised form in ordinary conversation? How common is this attitude among those you work with?

For the next week, set aside five or ten minutes a day to contemplate this attitude. See if you can concentrate on it gently but fully, so you penetrate to the heart of it. Repeat the exercise until you have the sense of a holding becoming loose or dissolving. Remember that challenging a negative attitude or role is a significant accomplishment that can help others as well as yourself. Look for tangible evidence of a shift in the way you are working and the results you are obtaining.

Exercise 53   Mirror Images

When you find yourself in a difficult or painful situation and can see no way out, a negative role may have you in its grip, so that it seems completely real to you. If you suspect that this is so, try telling the story of your difficulties out loud to a mirror. Do this for five minutes each evening. Watch the image in the mirror carefully—gestures, expressions, and tone of voice—and be especially sensitive to the different layers of feeling beneath the gestures. Awareness of these layers brings greater flexibility, allowing you to consciously shift your manifestation. This practice refines sensitivity to your deeper motivations and self-images, and will help you communicate clearly and honestly with others as well as with yourself.

Exercise 54   Opposition at the Back of the Mind

If you sense at the back of the mind a strong resistance to looking at a particular negative role or at negative roles in general, sit quietly for fifteen or twenty minutes and contemplate this opposition as fully as possible. What sensations and feelings arise in the body? What memories or images are stimulated? Can awareness touch these feelings and images directly? This exercise can be repeated as often as needed. You may wish to record your observations in your journal.

Exercise 55   Clearing Mistakes

Everyone accepts the idea that "We all make mistakes." But this means accepting that our awareness is too limited or cloudy to stay in touch with every part of the work we are doing.

Look back on several small mistakes you have made in the past week. For each one, recall as fully as possible your state of mind at the time. What was your mood? What emotions and stories were running through your head? How did they affect your awareness? Think through carefully how more awareness would have prevented the mistakes, and play off this imagined awareness against what you were feeling at the time, noting any tension and allowing it to dissolve. Note that the point is not to blame yourself for your mistakes, but to get clear on how they happen.

Exercise 56   Checking Satisfaction

Throughout the day, check on the level of your satisfaction as you work. Are you working with good cheer and good energy? With concentrated awareness? With confidence and dynamic motivation? Are

171

you free of emotional entanglements? Are you ready to meet challenges and overcome them moment by moment? Working well brings with it an intrinsic satisfaction, and if you dare to be honest with your-self, you will see that *any* negativity in your attitude indicates that you are wasting time or not perform-ing as well as you could.

Challenging Negativity

Full concentration on a negative attitude or role deepens our understanding of how the mind and senses operate. We see how mind reads its own contents and sets up dialogues. We observe how self-projection passes on information, images, and perceptions that are instantly referred to the structure of subject and object, supporting discrimination and separation. We grow sensitive to how images bring up feelings that are distributed throughout the body; how interpretations and comments create a kind of friction in the mind; how mind creates patterns of confusion and resistance that trap our energy and intelligence. We begin to notice that experiences of failure often have these features in common.

Concentrating fully on one negative role can show us a shadowy cast of characters that also turn up in other roles we play. There is 'the one who notices', 'the one who takes hold', 'the one who interprets', 'the slippery one who is hard to pin down', and others as well. As the observing mind catches up to each character, it can examine each one carefully, looking at it from all sides and up and down, always asking:

173

"Who are you? Where did you come from? What are you doing here? Why are you playing that role? How do you know that's so?"

If we ask these questions honestly and openly, we start to see the characters that inhabit our mind as ghostlike creations, woven out of images, thoughts, and feelings. The drama these characters enact begins to lose its hold. Do we really want to spend our time responding to this phantom barking and yapping, trapped only because we do not understand how the trap is made? What makes us cling to this way of being? Could we change?

The Power to Choose

If we let them, emotional dramas will occupy our minds from the moment we wake up in the morning until our last flickering thought at night, robbing our creativity and strength. Caught up in the illusion, we play our part. We give over our destiny to the play, honoring the terms of our engagement, which insist that the roles be played over and over. But the benefits we receive are limited. At times we may feel alive and important at being on stage; at times the drama of emotions may seem to create interest and excitement in our lives. More fundamentally, we may be relieved at not having to take a more active role in dealing with the difficulties we face, for emotional dramas place the responsibility for solving problems outside ourselves. But the price for turning away from responsibility is high: We renounce the power to determine whether we will succeed or fail in the goals we set for ourselves.

If we can see these dramas for what they are, we gain a new degree of freedom. When a voice whispers, "I can't do that," we can reply, "Who says so?" When the answer comes, "I say so! I know it!" we can again reply, "Who are you to tell me what I can and cannot do?" Whatever the excuses, the stories, or the dramas, there is no intrinsic reason to believe them or accept them as true.

As the playwright of our own dramas, we could write the play differently; we could even draw the curtain on the stage. Perhaps we are not ready to see through the old patterns entirely, but we can certainly ask ourselves whether we have to accept these stories of escape and limits and powerlessness. Here is one way to think about it: If we must manipulate ourselves, why not manipulate ourselves into something healthy and positive?

Choosing the Positive

It is time to turn to the positive: to begin caring enough to change. Once we have seen how we have been undermining our own ability to work successfully, we have a responsibility to ourselves and others not to fall back into old patterns. We need to find alternative ways of acting.

We know from experience that choosing positive action inspires and uplifts the spirit. It expands vision, builds strength and confidence, and leads to enduring accomplishment. Our stability, determination, and joyfulness attract others and support them in their work, so that a shared creative momentum builds toward success. This is a better way to work and live, and now is the time to choose it and put it into practice.

Each time we choose the positive, we reinforce our awareness that certain things need to change. By acting on this knowledge, we deepen our understanding of our experience. As positive energy begins to accumulate, our knowledge becomes embodied realization, developed in action.

We already know how to improve focus and how to give more energy to our work. We can act from this knowledge to strengthen positive patterns and increase our understanding, step by step. By continually cultivating our best knowledge, we can see more clearly how real change comes about. We can rely on this 'hands-on' knowledge with complete confidence and use it to cultivate success.

As we turn toward the positive, we must learn to guard our resolve, for old ways of acting have the addictive power of established habits. Again and again, they dance into the senses. So morning and evening and throughout the day we must generate the energy and disciplined focus that support transformation. We must learn to nurture the body and senses, encouraging them to relax and open, so that their positive energies can support a more balanced way of being.

Generating Positive Attitudes

Perhaps the idea of simply choosing the positive seems superficial—not connected to the real problems and obstacles we confront in our work. But this response is based on taking seriously the dramas we enact. If we can develop the focused concentration and awareness that let us see through these dramas, the problems we encounter in our work become less complicated and involved; many of them may disappear entirely. If the 'surface' of our experience can shift from negative to positive, why hold on to our commitment to the 'depths' of that experience? If we let go, what happens to our problems then?

Each time we refuse to indulge in excuses and procrastination, emotions and fantasies, we have more energy, concentration, and awareness to offer to our work. Each time we learn to stop a 'leak' in our energy, we can strengthen our concentration. Work becomes smoother and easier, and we settle naturally into the satisfying rhythms of productivity and enjoyment.

With a little discipline, a little encouragement for our own efforts, we can take on more responsibility for being genuinely positive. If life is like a drama, we can be like an actor trying out new roles. We can think the best thoughts we can imagine, take the best possible care of ourselves, and transform each and every one of our negative patterns.

Choosing the positive means turning toward knowledge and responsibility. Once we make this move we can engage each situation wholeheartedly, inviting insight and innovation, for we have nothing to protect or hide. The energy of learning that we invoke is active and creative, giving us the power to communicate clearly with others. The dynamic of growth opens a wide angle of opportunity. This way of working overcomes laziness, invigorates the sluggish mind, and drives out confusion and all forms of pettiness.

Because work is the proving ground and the occasion for developing this positive momentum, choosing the positive means being devoted to our work. But even though this may mean making intensive efforts over sustained periods of time, such dedication has nothing to do with the neurotic clinging of a workaholic. While the need to be busy mirrors the pain of dissatisfaction, a positive approach transforms negative pressures through fulfilling action. It rediscovers in dynamic, productive activity the path to appreciation and wholehearted enjoyment.

Imagine how creative and satisfying our lives would become if we used our awareness and energy to cultivate positive thoughts and memories, appreciative feelings, and calm, stable concentration. Simply by thinking well of others and ourselves, offering care and sensitivity and friendliness, and making a commitment to our own values and goals, we can inspire and activate positive energy and accomplishment. Deliberately feeding positivity to our mind and body, we can stimulate and support success.

Let us use the changeability of mind to our advantage. If we feel like creating a drama, let us create a positive drama! At any moment, we can restore the sparkle to our eyes and the cheer to our manner. We are free to try anything, think anything, and be anything. Knowing this is so, let us imbue our lives with awareness, concentration, and energy, preparing the way for faith, commitment, and loyalty.

Exercise 57   Building Positivity

Pick a time each day to perform the following simple ceremony: In whatever manner you wish, make a formal promise to yourself not to submit to negativity, but to turn again and again to the positive. Perhaps the morning is best, so that your intention informs the whole day. Or you may prefer to wait until evening, when you have more negative material to work with. Once you have picked a time, do this ceremony daily for at least two weeks, looking for some small ritual that will make your commitment very alive and real.

As you renew your promise, watch for negative internal messages such as "I'm sorry," "I'm frightened," "I'm worried," "I'm inadequate," "I'm incompetent," "I'm guilty." Note how they restrain energy and reduce awareness. The challenge is to see the negativity clearly without submitting to the emotional drama that supports it, and to shift again and again to clear awareness, deeper concentration, and supportive energy.

Exercise 58   Nourishing Images

Set aside a few moments each hour to nourish yourself with images you love, thoughts that uplift you, and feelings of appreciation for a beautiful or worthwhile aspect of your work. Make the extra effort to make your workspace a clean and inviting environment. By letting awareness touch beauty in the space around you during the day, you can activate a feeling of clarity and spaciousness that deeply nourishes the heart.

Exercise 59   Guarding Against Negativity

The arising of negativity and resistance is an early warning that we must be alert to guard our commitment and clarity.

A. *At the Beginning*   The most important time to check for the arising of subtle negative patterns is right at the beginning of a difficult challenge. At such moments, ask yourself: Am I renouncing my awareness so that I do not have to think about the obstacles I face? Am I wasting or blocking my energy so that experience does not become too vivid and possibly overwhelming? Am I letting concentration remain out of focus to guarantee that my responsibilities will stay vague and shapeless?

B. *Dislike*   Train yourself to catch attitudes of dislike toward your work or business, toward maintaining discipline, or toward authority at an early stage, before they become justifications for laziness and procrastination.

C. *Sliding By*   Whenever you do not want to work or are tempted to let a commitment slide by, set off an inner alarm. What is really going on? React with suspicion when you feel like not bothering about something or when you come up with reasons for not doing your best or accepting mediocre results.

D. *Resistance* If you are in a position of leadership, watch out when you resist doing what you know needs to be done. Clarify and challenge the roles played out in the inner dialogues that run through your mind. Look to see if you are hiding, and be on the lookout for excuses that cover up the hiding and prevent you from waking up.

Exercise 60 Strengthening the Positive

A. *Just 5%* Resolve to give just 5% more energy to your work this week. Notice any difference in your results, and trace out how this happened. Next week give another 5%. Perhaps in a month you might be giving 15% more than before. Consider the difference this could make in just a few months.

B. *Strengthening Focus* Today and for the rest of the month, resolve to focus better hour by hour. Find a way to remind yourself of this resolve from time to time as you work. Reflect back at the end of the day to see how successful you have been. Note any differences in your results.

C. *Positive Atmosphere* While working, cultivate a cheerful manner, a pleasant voice, and a humorous warmth that helps to create a positive atmosphere. By employing kind words and gestures and paying attention to the mood and tone of inner experience, you can improve the quality of each day for yourself and for everyone you deal with. Do this for two weeks or a month; by then it may have become natural.

D. *Evaluating Results* Each week for the next month, set aside time at the close of the week to evaluate the results you have achieved in your work. What positive contributions have you made? Look in terms of plans, scheduling, clear communication, and encouragement to yourself and others, as well as goals you have met and the quality of your work.

Exercise 61   Charting Attitudes

The chart on the following page lists attitudes identified with high levels of awareness, concentration, and energy (left-hand column), as well as their opposites (right-hand column). Photocopy enough copies of this chart to last for two weeks.

Consider each attitude as it relates to yourself, your co-workers, your work, your tools, your materials, your clients or customers, your competitors, and your organization. Twice each day for the next week, check and see which attitudes predominate. Use colored pencils or pens to distinguish checks made at the two times. Practice the exercise for two weeks, noting the results at the end of each week in a neutral way.

Exercise 62   Exercising New Patterns

For the next week, try changing one or more basic ways you have of acting so that they express a more

Specific Patterns

Date_____ Time _____ Time _____

Satisfaction	Complaints
Taking responsibility	Making excuses
Presence	Fantasies
Willingness	Resentment
Silent space	Storytelling
Not ignoring	Hiding
Giving forth	Holding back
Cutting through	Logical figuring
Moving into action	Doubt and hesitating
Organized work	Wandering around
Using intelligence	Blindly accepting
Gentle and kind	Harsh and critical
Encouraging	Destructive
Upholding the positive	Disrespectful
Sympathetic	Isolated
Joyful	Depressed
Creative	Uninspired
Future vision	Stuck in present
Clear on cause & effect	Stuck in past
Recognizing fantasy	Stuck in future
Tuned to all senses	Stuck in head
Independent	Caught in emotion
Hearing meaning	Caught in words
Seeing depth	Caught in images

positive outlook; for instance, the way you talk or walk, what you eat or wear, where you go, what you do with your free time, the tone of your voice, or the posture of your body. Experiment lightly, without being too serious. Note your positive results at the end of the week and let them inspire you to keep on experimenting.

Waking Up
to Goodness

There are many ways to stimulate appreciation for the positive flavors of direct experience. When the sun is shining and the world is illumined with beautiful light, we can fill our hearts with joy. Others who are living or dying today may not have the same opportunity to experience the beauty of light and life. Why not savor our good fortune in having this chance?

Small opportunities for appreciation in our work environment can open our hearts and awaken our senses: a single beautiful flower, a picture, a clean and well-ordered work space. Whenever we enjoy the beauty around us, we can expand the positive feelings that arise, distributing them throughout the body and into the space around us.

We can treat our thoughts in the same way. When positive images or ideas quicken sensations in the body, we can let these feelings warm our hearts and clear our heads. Positive thoughts linked to what has real value will not cheat or fool us, mislead us or draw us into confusion. They offer dynamic power and encouragement and bring us close to inner knowledge.

If we give ourselves a chance to develop the positive feeling tones in our bodies and minds, we discover that the senses are an unlimited source of inner wealth. There is no need to turn to drugs or seek out sex, romance, or other diversions to shift our consciousness out of its routine. Cultivating the positive flavors in ordinary experience is actually far more rewarding, because these feelings and sensations open the door to our own heart.

By strengthening positive attitudes, we also strengthen our ability to turn away from unproductive patterns of behavior. For example, when we can give ourselves time to appreciate our experience and accomplishments, we will no longer waste time in daydreams. When we learn to experience real gratitude for our accomplishments, we naturally ask how we can contribute further. Instead of pursuing our own private pleasures, we cultivate enjoyment as a natural part of our work.

Extending Positive Time

Positive experiences have great beauty, but they often seem to last only a few brief moments. By skillfully exercising awareness and concentration, we can challenge this limitation, learning to extend the duration of positive experience.

Whenever positive feelings arise, we can use the power of concentration to prolong the rich sensations and enjoy them more deeply. When they start to disappear, focused awareness can help us recapture and enjoy them again. We can treasure the precious moments when our spirit is light and our mind open, letting them uplift our hearts like the joy of a smile or the special intimacy of a loving glance. We can invite the richness of this pleasure to dwell as an honored guest in our innermost heart.

When we think of all the frustrations and obstacles we encounter at work, cultivating and extending what is positive may seem unrealistic. But this is only because we do not realize that the routine experiences of daily work can be a source of deep and lasting delight. This approach is no gimmick, nor is it just an exercise to try for a few minutes. Learning to extend positive time is a valuable step in training the mind that can transform our capacities and our ability to accomplish what we value. Why not set aside all the reasons for rejecting this strategy out of hand and see what happens when we try?

Start by simply imagining that you really can extend positive experience in this way: By imagining positive energy, you ready a place for it. As the image grows stronger, you may feel actual body sensations, perhaps warmth or heat. Negative thoughts and feelings may arise to prevent you from continuing, but instead of accepting these judgments and feelings as true, let the lightness and warmth of the positive gently touch them and release the tension gathered within them. Soon you will learn how to make a home for the positive in your heart.

Greater awareness and the power of imagination can also help to shorten negative experiences. For example, if you feel hopelessly stuck in your present situation, you can remind yourself that time is always moving and changing. You can imagine a different time and place, in which the knowledge you need to transform your situation is freely available. You can build confidence and develop the courage to act by remembering past times of difficulty that eventually shifted and changed. Finally, you can draw on knowledge gained from past experiences to interpret and understand what is happening now.

Enjoying Time

When we enjoy our positive feelings and thoughts, the light of awareness clears and brightens, concentration becomes more focused and steady, and the rhythm of energy stabilizes at a new, higher level. Our bodily and mental energies become more balanced and our way of thinking richer, and our creativity expresses itself in new patterns of action and new initiatives. Our enjoyment and growing sensitivity open time, allowing us to relax 'into' time and incorporate it into our lives. The rich energies and sensations that time makes available allow the diamond key of awareness to open the gateway to relaxation. Time and energy join in a union that deepens appreciation of positive thoughts and feelings, revealing deeper dimensions of satisfaction.

The quality of this satisfaction can be a strong support, especially during stressful times when negative thoughts and feelings begin to bombard the senses. Without any quality of forcing and without needing to be asked, awareness invites the senses to be more sensitive and is invited into the senses in turn. Comfortable and open, awareness is simply aware, without taking any fixed positions. There is no need to try, to interfere, or to make an effort. Applied to work, this open awareness manifests in an almost 'doing nothing' way of working. It assures that work will lead us deeper into our own being. Light and free, filled with appreciation, confident and creative, we can discover endless opportunities to work effectively for what has value. Fulfillment becomes inseparable from accomplishment, and success in what we do is virtually assured.

Abundance of Positive Knowledge

Even when our focus is on success in work, our first responsibility is to take care of ourselves. This means learning to rely on inner knowledge, a kinder and more reliable guide than any friend or counselor. Inner knowledge teaches us to strengthen positive attitudes, cultivate enjoyment, and protect our awareness so that the mind does not undermine itself with negative emotions and thoughts.

When we use work as the vehicle for refining awareness, concentration, and energy, we develop such inner knowledge naturally, and we soon discover its enduring value for ourselves and others. If we make the growth of this knowledge our goal, this higher purpose shines through the specific purposes that inform our work; it is there whether we acknowledge it consciously or not.

189

The inner knowledge of how to develop human resources is abundantly positive; we can give it away to others without any loss to ourselves. As we care for ourselves, we can also serve, help, lead, and counsel others. Life and work become a dynamic unity that has intrinsic power and is inherently rewarding.

When work becomes the gateway to knowledge, whatever we do is meaningful and creative. Each day is an invitation to accomplishment, a spring garden fertile with new seeds that can sprout into beautiful flowers. Tending this garden is an ongoing delight, and responding to each new challenge only deepens our pleasure. Skillfully creating beauty and bringing our investment of time and energy to fruition, we can enrich our lives and share the harvest of our accomplishment with others.

Waking Up to Goodness

Today many people are trying to bring human society into better balance with the environment. Valuable as these efforts are, the goal at which they aim only hints at the treasures that await us. Beyond the beauty of nature, beyond the beauty of art and music and science, there is the beauty of goodness. The vision of goodness can be a powerful force motivating us to change through our work.

Today the notion of goodness is out of favor. There are few living examples of people who express basic goodness in their every action, and not many people understand how to use their work and livelihood as positive forces in the world. Yet the fundamentals of a kind heart and basic human strength and stability have not lost their potency. In the new world order that is presently emerging, where the old traditions hold little power, each of us can contribute to goodness by developing our own inner resources and enacting a positive way to be.

The commitment to self-inquiry, self-reflection, and self-development gives us all the tools we need to make a real contribution. Whether we choose to act on this opportunity is up to us. We are our own witness of how we use time, awareness, and knowledge; no one else is watching or inspecting. When we draw on what we know is best and dedicate ourselves to a higher purpose, our good intention brings warmth and sincerity to our heart and to the deeper levels of our consciousness, sustaining our efforts from day to day for as long as we live. Our presence becomes a living example, our willingness and responsibility an active meditation on the welfare of all humanity.

Each morning, we can decide to offer whatever we have and do for the benefit of others. As we work, we can express our resolve by giving knowledge, determination, and energy from the gut level. When we interact with others, we can be sensitive to their needs and encourage their positive growth. At the end of the day we can bring this sense of wholeness to a satisfying close.

There are questions we can ask that let us picture the accomplishments we wish to achieve and taste their inner significance. "How can I help?" "What are my deepest purposes?" "What do I wish to contribute to the world?" Contemplating these questions, keeping them alive in our hearts, we can renew our vision and inspiration. By appreciating our vision deeply, we naturally begin to imagine the future unfolding toward the present, and specific goals and actions take form in our mind. Then we can give our best to our work, confident that it will return to us a sweet satisfaction that inspires us to give more. Our generosity will flow in a circuit that generates more satisfaction, more appreciation, and more dedication.

Exercise 63   Stimulating New Vision

Exercises that balance the breath, lighten thoughts, and open the heart can help to open up new vision, taking it beyond fantasy and imagination into real embodiment. For several such exercises, see *Kum Nye Relaxation*, Part 1, pp. 35–54, 153–55, and 168–69.

Exercise 64   Recording Intention

Make time to visit a quiet place in nature where you can share your good feelings with space and time, with the rocks and trees. Reflecting on the work you are doing, acknowledge and enjoy the results you have already achieved, and quietly dedicate your knowledge and positive energies to your friends and to good causes and purposes, strengthening your intention to improve your contribution. When the time feels right, speak from your innermost heart, recording aloud your intention to make your best effort from this moment forward.

Exercise 65 Extending Positive Time

For a few minutes every day, gently relax tension in your body and look for positive, nourishing feelings. Expand these feelings, letting them pass deeply into the body. Distribute feelings of joyful lightness to every part of the body, letting them heal any doubts, hesitations, and tensions that may be present.

PART FOUR

Waking Up
for the World

Opening Time
through Awareness

We all have the capacity to embody visions of knowledge and shape reality in different ways. Work is a vehicle for refining this capacity, and learning to use our work well can help us contact our purpose in being alive.

There is a wonderful enjoyment in this way of working—like falling in love for the first time. It is the enjoyment of a heart overflowing with a light, awakened quality that accompanies us wherever we go and whatever we do.

The way to activate this enjoyment is through developing awakened mind, using it to mine the depths of human consciousness and claim its manifold treasures. Awareness, concentration, and energy, our most precious resources, are the means for accomplishing this. Once we have realized their true worth, we can never settle for less than bringing them to fulfillment.

The knowledge of how to use awareness, concentration, and energy can be applied to any worthwhile purpose. The results we obtain will testify to the accuracy and power of our understanding, and our example will inspire others who are searching for better ways to lead successful lives.

In the first three parts of this book, we have looked at various ways in which awareness, concentration, and energy contribute to our work and can be activated within any working situation. Now we will investigate a way of working that goes deeper, opening up the vast creativity of knowledge and making it available for a new level of accomplishment. If you have already worked with the exercises and approaches presented in the earlier parts of this book and are motivated to go further, you may find this more advanced material valuable.

Refining Knowledge of Time

As always, the natural starting point for refining awareness, concentration, and energy is time. Human life is so closely linked to time that when we find new ways of connecting awareness with the temporal flow, we move naturally to a new level of achievement and responsibility.

Although the study of time is a complex topic, and going deeply into it would require more careful investigation, there is a first level of refinement in our relationship to time that we can undertake and master now. By sharpening awareness, strengthening concentration, and stabilizing energy, we can learn to touch time and extend time, cutting through the obstacles that prevent us from waking up further.

We can start by developing our ability to extract the most positive accomplishments we can from our time and our work. Such practice can become the gateway to a second level of mastery, where specific techniques are transcended. At this level, knowledge emerges spontaneously, and time itself provides the energy that fuels refinement and expansion.

The initial steps toward mastery of time have been introduced already. We can choose to be on top of time, scheduling our activities, strengthening our discipline, and appreciating the value of each moment. We can bring awareness to time, going deeply into experience in ways that open up limitless new possibilities.

Touched by awareness, time expands, allowing us to do two things at once. Simultaneously creating and focusing on what we experience, we can relax into each event, like a painter enjoying the act of painting or a musician hearing in his mind the sound of the score that he is reading.

The more awareness opens, the more time opens, revealing new dimensions of awareness. Mind and senses interact, painting beautiful art on the canvas of time. Creativity continues unpatterned, creating new and elegant patterns. Innovative knowledge enriches body and mind: Embodied directly in our work, it offers opportunities and challenges that help us make the best use of our abilities.

The creative interplay of time and awareness blesses us with abundance. With the power of time on our side, we can share energy and love with others, creating mutual joy and confidence. Each one of us can be a hero, inspiring others and ourselves. Transcending all sense of poverty or of being trapped by limitations, we can work joyfully toward our most cherished goals, full of confidence in our ability to achieve our aims.

Releasing the Pressure of Time

When awareness and concentration are unable to contact time, the pressure of time manifests in our work in a very particular way. Each moment is marked off by sharp edges, and each edge hooks up to the next, generating an ever-increasing momentum. The force of this momentum turns moments of time into tiny points, each of which strike consciousness like a blow.

Our reaction to this circumstance is predictable. We become anxious and impulsive, unable to see clearly what actions are advisable or what their consequences will be. Our decisions lead to mistakes, and work does not go smoothly. Bombarded by streams of thoughts, memories, and images, the senses close down. Our rational powers go unused; our intuition loses contact with the situation and with other people's psychology. Unable to bring our inner resources to bear on the onrushing flow of time, we have few choices: We jump to conclusions; we pull back; we turn our attention elsewhere. Emotions flare up easily, and minor difficulties quickly escalate out of control.

If we were able to concentrate more fully at these times, time would feed back to us the knowledge we need to make better decisions. But concentration depends on awareness for direction, and awareness can guide concentration only if it can first contact and accommodate time by expanding each moment.

Through exercising awareness in advance, making plans and forecasts and evaluating the consequences of our actions, we can offer ourselves some protection against being caught off balance when time starts to accelerate and pressures build. From this basis, we can develop awareness as a resource that supports concentration even when the pressure of time becomes intense.

A focused awareness can touch and expand time by relying on its own stable momentum to counteract the overwhelming power of the usual temporal dynamic. Soft, almost visionary, awareness can turn each moment of time into an occasion, allowing concentration room to operate. If we imagine each point of time as the apex of a triangle, this shift in awareness would be like opening up the triangle, much as a flower opens in blossoming.

Instead of jumping here and there, like someone flipping through the pages of a photograph album without registering their contents, focused awareness can take events in fully, registering their features and their relationships to other events. Leaving footprints behind as it passes from one moment to the next, awareness can fully record the knowledge contained within each moment, preserving it for the future.

Alert and loose, a soft and focused awareness can see through the surface of the events that time presents, broadly aware of sense impressions and contributing circumstances. Radar-like in its sensitivity, it can maintain a distanced perspective while at the same time being fully embodied. Its illumined quality ripples out at the edges of each thought or image, radiating a light that is not centered on thought or captured by thought. When thoughts and emotions flash like patches of fire, awareness can enfold them, checking their headlong speed. As we learn to balance this awareness skillfully, allowing its inner qualities to become lighter, we find that we have the ability to manifest full concentration that is luminous and open. Guided by awareness, such concentration lets us penetrate time's pressure and make use of its energy.

Exercise 66   Awareness Beyond Thought

Ordinarily, we imagine that awareness arises within thoughts and perceptions, but awareness can also operate without being confined in this way. Just as light can radiate through space without having to be linked to a specific source, so awareness can operate beyond the fixed boundaries of what we perceive or think about. When we cultivate this more dynamic, unbounded awareness, we leave old temporal structures behind. The following exercise can help familiarize you with this shift.

Pick a time when you are relaxed, and notice each thought as it arises. Look for a halo of awareness around the thought, associated with it but not involving the thought's content. This means finding a point of balanced distance from the thought, something like the point in a magnetic field where the pull of the field can be felt but its force does not irresistibly attract its object.

Once you discover this halo of awareness, you can invite its presence without reference to the thought or the activity of thinking. Doing this requires a delicate touch. As soon as you tell yourself to be aware, you impose a limit on the natural radiance of awareness; as soon as you look for awareness as an object, you renew perception's fixed juxtapositions; as soon as you describe or explain the appearance of awareness, you turn its luminosity into a featureless and barren blankness.

The alternative to these self-contradicting approaches is to let the light quality of awareness itself become the gateway to awareness. You can proceed gently, balancing the subject-object polarities of thought, touching this light quality gradually and very subtly. It will manifest as a relaxing and released quality, as 'waking up, can't describe it, living in the center of the mind, opening the center of the heart'.

Bringing Knowledge to Time

It is when light enters awareness that awareness is able to open the sharp points of time and restore to experience the balance that supports full concentration. Within full concentration, light reveals the rich quality of awareness inseparable from the depth of knowledge. The effect is to instantly liberate mind from the rigid limits of thoughts and perceptions.

The liberating quality of this contemplation changes the quality of the will, freeing up the forceful, negative aspects of fixed positions. Psychological tensions and ways of acting, as well as orientations to life and time and to our sense of self, all lighten up. A wealth of knowledge releases us from confusion and dissatisfaction.

As we learn to distribute the light quality of awareness into concentration, we can discover within each moment a way of working and acting that allows ample opportunity for insight, appreciation, and intelligence. Through the opening of time, the tensions that come from time's momentum lighten, and the senses come back into contact with experience. As awareness continues to deepen, we hear sounds differently and see with new eyes; we discover a subtle, tasty new food that can nourish the body and mind.

The ground of this new experience is the new availability of knowledge in time, made possible by the lightness of awareness. When each moment does not rush by breathlessly, concentration can hold experience open for knowledge to enter. Ultimately, we can discover vast new spaces within what was once a single moment of time. Here a boundless body of knowledge is present and active. Without guidance, without a teacher, we can study this knowledge and become one with it.

Through this transformation, work naturally takes on a spiritual quality largely missing in business today. Invited by time, awareness and concentration interact with knowledge, steadily deepening. Our sense of purpose strengthens and our sense of frustration disappears. Without having to forcefully change the way we operate or the standards that guide our conduct, we act in ways that are more productive and also more balanced.

Exercise 67   Extending Invitation

Compared to our ordinary ways of perceiving and knowing, the light of awareness is quite subtle, and you may not be able to contact it within daily experience until you have more experience with relaxation. However, you can start right now to explore the special quality of invitation that opens the depths of awareness to light.

To experiment with ways to bring this quality into whatever you are doing, focus on lightening up whatever is forceful, emphatic, and well-established. Do this in playful ways. For instance, you could move differently; you could speak or even breathe differently; you could make a decision in a new way. You could invite others to participate in unexpected ways; you could invite new sensations.

Once you have some experience with this playful lightness, invite awareness to contact time directly, even if you do not really know how this could happen. Invite more concentration into awareness or more energy into concentration. Explore in any way you wish, inviting new ways of inviting.

Do this exercise for a week and then evaluate the outcome. Reflect on your experience and decide on any modifications. Continue for at least another week. When you feel ready, look for an occasion when you feel pressured at work. As you continue working, extend an open invitation to light to enter awareness, free from the forms of thoughts and perceptions. Then invite this luminous awareness into time and into your situation as a whole. What is the impact on your ability to concentrate? Your ability to find creative solutions to your difficulties?

Welcoming Fulfillment

Once we stand in a different relationship to time, we can enjoy work at a new level. The next step in refining our relationship to work is to cultivate this quality of enjoyment. We can do this by developing a new level of relaxation, allowing awareness to expand into the fullness of time, where deep enjoyment resides.

As we approach this second level of relaxation, instructions to pay attention to body, mind, and senses are set aside as being based on a kind of subtle fixation and manipulation of experience. The awareness that opens through this relaxation is not based on attention or intention. It is lighter and more inviting than ordinary awareness, more receptive to light and more accommodating. Gentle and calm, accepting and allowing, it opens and dissolves intention. Gradually the fixed juxtapositions that are the usual agents of the instructor-mind relax. There is no telling or being told, no being taught, no fixing firmly through perception. Without losing strength, motivation becomes looser, more accepting of the fullness of experience.

207

Awareness at this level is closely present, but we do not own or possess it. As effortlessly as a mirror or a pane of glass, awareness quietly reflects the position of the subject as the carrier of awareness and the position of awareness as the property of the subject. Awareness openly welcomes this twofold reflection of subject and object, and the reflection in turn relaxes further, feeding relaxation back to awareness.

Treasury of the Senses

This looser, relaxed awareness becomes a gateway for the senses. Now it is the turn of the senses to relax, releasing warmth into the sensations of the body. This developing warmth extends a new invitation that continues on and on. A gentle feeling opens in the heart center, soft and warm; in some people this feeling moves easily to the throat and head centers, or to the crown center at the top of the head.

As each center opens up, the ongoing invitation is magnified. The senses respond, enriching the flavor of experience. Mind and body become still, allowing the flame of the senses to burn more brightly, and sense experience becomes deeply and fully satisfying, nurturing and beneficial. Enjoyment opens awareness; awareness allows the senses to open still further, until even the cells of the body open. Deeply pleasurable sensations come: The invitation has been accepted and the guest arrives. These abundant sensations can be further developed and extended, increasing joy and happiness for as long as we wish.

Through daily practice, mind can learn to accommodate the willingness and openness that yield these abundant treasures of the senses. The more we can listen, see, touch, and be, the more we encourage our life to become richer and fuller.

This learning process becomes a model of self-mastery, allowing us to profit from our own sources of knowledge. Cherishing ourselves and sharing what we cherish with others, we discover benefits that fill the gap in our lives. The unique beauty of this fullness can manifest in creative action that reveals the mysteries of daily life. With further training, we can learn to extend these sensations and let them flow throughout all of consciousness, making available the full Body of Knowledge.

To awaken this special relaxation, practice gently and carefully, but not too carefully. We are accustomed to being taught and led, and our intellect—closed to our heart of hearts—does not know how to touch our spirit directly. But there is a way: Pronounce without sound, touch without movement, see without looking. When you know how to do this, being can operate fully and dynamically—better than ever before. This is not an empty promise: The results are there to be witnessed, and they encourage a knowledge that fulfills human being and supports the highest values. The sources lie close at hand, in the treasury of the human senses and feelings.

Developing
Concentration

As the body and mind relax more fully, energy released from emotional patterns and the binding power of inner dialogues becomes available to support concentration and align itself with knowledge. Balanced and made more open through relaxation, awareness can direct both concentration and energy in new ways. Reminding, encouraging, allowing, suggesting, and advising, awareness supports the deepening of concentration into the fullness of contemplation.

The 'feel' or energetic power of full concentration melts seeing into a precious liquid that dissolves obstructions to the mind's natural power of perception. This energy of contemplation can be used to further mine the treasures of consciousness. The knowledge it gives access to has been used throughout the ages to open up vision and skillfully bring forth alternative solutions to human difficulties.

Full Availability

Through full concentration, the energy of mind is released from bouncing back and forth within repetitive patterns. Refreshed, preserved, and increased, the abundant, self-generating energy of mind catches time. Sponsored and directed by awareness and available through concentration, energy and time bring forth action and accomplishment. Mind is free to carry on with full efficiency, for energy and time are more than sufficient. Knowledge and creativity are plentiful, and they too can be exercised and manifested in accomplishment. Though inevitably limited when described in words and images, this creative activity is in fact pervasive.

Applied to the domain of work, contemplation brings mind into harmony with the contents of the work being done. Energy and action are so unified there is no possibility of conflict between them. Each moment of experience is inspiring. There is no being tired, no dislike of work. We experience work as a manifestation of energy that is our very nature.

Through deepening concentration in our work, we can develop the subtle inner qualities of mind with ever-increasing skill. As awareness moves deeper into the mind, the vastness of mind and body awaken and become more aware. The sharpness of awareness lightens, contributing to our ability to extend time and allowing us to develop a way of seeing that is both sensitive and accurate. Lighter awareness in turn lightens the bubbling activity of mind. Sensitive, fresh, and alive, the mind feeds back to awareness subtle and deeply interesting projections. As awareness delicately explores these sophisticated manifestations of mind, there are manifold transformations: Energy becomes time, time becomes awareness, and

211

awareness opens concentration into the fullness of contemplation.

Within contemplation, awareness and concentration jointly carry on this seeing and being aware, continuing what is already single-minded. As the experience of being is extended in time, we can mine the environment of mind for the hidden riches of awareness, concentration, and energy.

As the refined and subtle part of awareness becomes full, complete, and open, contemplation opens up more room in space. The allowing unboundedness of space gives further extension to time, balancing, energizing, and enriching experience and the quality of the senses. The inner light of awareness transforms the sensitive rhythms of mind and the movement of moments of time, completely balancing attitudes such as anxiety and rashness.

Mind engaging work at these levels involves itself with time in a playful and truly enjoyable way. There is still the quality of focusing on work—and reminders to reinforce focusing may be needed—but presence itself becomes dynamic, opening mind to ever increasing dimensions of awareness, concentration, and energy.

Only the initial experiences of this contemplation can bring this description to life and make it available to the presence of mind. The words used here, such as 'mind' and 'light', are only tools, their usefulness restricted by the necessary structure of pointing 'from' something 'to' something. At a deeper level of experiencing, when explanation is no longer needed, more expressive vocabularies may emerge.

How to Develop Contemplation

Mind can promote contemplation at any time, making it a part of daily work and life. Once one thought has been extended through full concentration, other thoughts or sense perceptions can be extended as well. As we improve our understanding of how to exercise awareness, concentration, and energy, contemplation occurs naturally.

To develop contemplation as we work, we can bring awareness to time, awareness to energy, and awareness to awareness. We can put energy into energy, energy into time, and energy into concentration. We can concentrate on awareness, concentrate on time, and concentrate on concentration. Each day we can choose whatever aspect we find most suitable or consider lacking. Whatever we are doing, at any time, we can continue with this active refinement.

As we develop sensitive ways to practice, awareness records them in memory, preserving for mind the knowledge they embody. As we perfect our inner qualities, they likewise come together in mind and are preserved in awakened awareness. Awareness becomes so open and sensitive that it registers recognition of experience directly. Unfolding of its own accord, awareness records, carries on, and becomes more perfected, making knowledge available without any special effort to recall or remember.

As contemplation extends its influence and awareness develops greater capacity, we forget less frequently and make fewer mistakes. Awareness in its opening makes available the energy of mind, and the aura of awareness that surrounds the will or force of mind, a key source for its dynamic power, is generated automatically. Awareness registers with almost photographic precision, and awareness of awareness condenses into concentration, refining awareness of awareness further.

Within the full concentration of contemplation, nothing is burdensome or constricted. Concentration is broad, pervasive, and light. There is a sense of freshness, like airing out a stuffy room, a sense of everything being cleared up and renewed. A solid balance develops, not physical but nevertheless utterly stable. We can begin to say: "Here is basic grounding; here is being."

This quality of a foundation cleansed of all obscurations and obstacles is the peak of contemplation. Within it there can be no distractions, for awareness sees pervasively whatever is coming, just as we see an approaching plane on the far horizon.

Contemplation is like a cleansing initiation for the stuffy mind of emotionality. Clearing the mind of dullness, it awakens the mind from confusion and the causes of confusion. Mining the treasure of this awakened mind, we cannot lose or waste time and energy, for our actions lead spontaneously to creative accomplishment. Sharp and clear, undistracted and balanced, we can direct our attention both inward and outward. The senses offer rich enjoyment and the mind develops the full capacities necessary for leadership.

Exercise 68   Energy of Contemplation

Sit quietly and hold energy in the belly, resisting the temptation to release it through emotions or restless thoughts. You will find that thoughts become sharper and the senses more vibrant. Bring these qualities to bear on difficult issues connected with work. As perception brightens and judgments improve, you can cut through confusion and arrive at better decisions. You can use this exercise to penetrate resistance and accomplish more.

To engage this rich energy of contemplation during the day, take a moment to sit or stand quietly and generate energy in the belly by holding it with light tension. Contemplate the belly until a feeling of warmth arises; then, without releasing the tension, holding it lightly, continue with your work.

Exercise 69   Understanding Interactions

As you develop the practice of contemplation, apply it to explore the active interplay of awareness, concentration, and energy. Consider, for example, these possible connections:

Awareness of awareness leads to insight.
Concentration on awareness leads to illumination.
Energy applied to awareness leads to clarity.

Can you confirm these interactions in your own experience? What are the results when awareness, concentration, and energy are each applied to concentration? To energy? What happens when awareness, concentration, and energy are fully integrated and the result is applied to each factor in turn? How do awareness, concentration, and energy open time? What is their relationship to the inner structures of knowledge?

Hold these questions in your mind and apply the power of contemplation to their investigation. It may take some time and considerable experience to arrive at deeper understanding in this way, but if you are patient, your confidence in exploration will increase. If you do not feel after some time that you are making any progress, set the questions aside and return to them at a later time.

Light of Knowledge

Supported by concentration and energy that deepen toward being fully embodied, awareness wakes up to time. As it touches time directly, and time opens to receive it, a fundamental transformation occurs: Like a spring bubbling up from a crevice in a rocky mountain slope, knowledge pours forth its abundance, hinting at great treasures beyond our present imagination.

Drawing on this knowledge, awareness can excavate time further, finding deep within time powerful energies that allow experience to manifest in completely new patterns. As we tap this knowledge, we learn to move with time, delighting in its rhythms and patterns. Gradually we learn to take command of its potential.

Innovative Knowledge

Knowledge is the source of knowledge. As our investigations teach us to read the mind and deepen awareness, we activate this dynamic power of knowledge, which encompasses both theory and practical applications. Not limited to one field of expertise or another, we can experiment creatively, tracing the Body of Knowledge and tapping rich realms of deepening satisfaction.

Once we have awakened to knowledge, knowledge becomes our intimate companion, our partner—the keyholder and treasure bearer that freely offers up its treasures to our inquiry. By testing and refining understanding, we experience directly for ourselves how knowledge works. In time we find knowledge in our hands and in our voice; we know it so closely that there is no need to seek it or even give it names. As the purpose of our work becomes embodied, the Body of Knowledge becomes our path. Our practice of awareness and mindfulness in our work brings forth innovative understanding. New goals and new visions become spontaneously available, opening new possibilities for all humanity.

Transforming Dance of Knowledge

Cultivating knowledge, perfecting what is imperfect, developing our intelligence and capacities, we human beings have come a long way, passing through all kinds of errors. But there is still much work to be done. Now is the time to challenge the limitations of our own energy and mind, looking steadily for better ways to activate concentration and energy and increase our productivity. There are countless new ways to stimulate body energy and positive imagination, increase awareness, and activate a healthy, refreshing, and wholesome quality of life.

Because it is based on our experience, our understanding of what is positive and valuable is clear and reliable, and gives purpose to our lives. This knowing will not confuse us or deceive us into ignorance. It is the truth on which we can take our stand.

Applying this knowledge to every aspect of our lives, we can lighten and transform our body, our emotions, our voice, our intentions, and our thoughts; we can express this transformation in all that we do. Confident that we have something of great value and beauty to offer, we can begin a playful and creative dance with awareness, concentration, and energy.

Seeing our positive actions and sensing our positive thoughts and feelings, others are naturally drawn to the same path. We can respond with intelligence and caring, for we know how to resolve our own problems and deal with our own difficulties. We can readily make the problems of others our own and take responsibility to promote knowledge for their sake.

Creating Positive Energy

Once we have made a fundamental connection to knowledge, darkness, mistakes, and ignorance no longer need to be obstacles to the process of transformation. Seeing the source of our limitations in the past, we understand how knowledge can transform limits now and in the future. We awaken to a vision of the radiant light of knowledge illuminating our own heart and encouraging others to experience the beauty of ever-manifesting space and time.

In charge of our lives at last, we can be responsible for charging our thoughts, images, sensations, and feelings with positive energy. We can activate appreciation, grateful for positive thoughts and feelings, for encouragement, for our inner resources, for the aliveness of our senses, and for appreciation itself. We can give thanks for this splendid life, this magical body, this beautifully intricate mind.

Appreciation deepens into intimacy with life itself, in an embrace more profound than any physical gesture. So deep is this intimate appreciation for the gift of life that the feelings it generates are almost visible. We love and delight and enjoy ourselves with a vibrant dancing energy. No longer do we need to hold onto the hopeless view that sees time, energy, and knowledge as being in short supply. Space is big enough to make room for shortages; time is full enough to open infinite opportunities for knowledge.

All of us together can join in dancing and celebrating this bright opportunity. No matter what has happened until now, our chances are not lost. Together we can create a positive point of view; together we can cultivate the abundance of knowledge.

Once we give knowledge a field of action in which to operate and practice, knowledge refines itself naturally. As our perspective deepens through the exercise of leadership, we can stand on our realization that knowledge supports compassion, true responsibility, and discipline. Sustained and nourished by compassion, knowledge grows and flourishes, blossoms and bears abundant fruit: the perfection of all positive qualities and the accomplishment of all beneficial actions. We can be confident that our commitment to heal the disorder of our minds and the pain of our hearts will have positive results. Knowing that this opportunity is there, and seeing how precious life is, we act spontaneously to contribute knowledge to the universe.

Acting for Humanity

Now our endeavors emerge from a different dimension. Wishing to be of benefit, we open our hearts and minds to humanity. Although the practice of compassion and loving kindness toward all may be too exalted to make our own, our resolve to bring more light into the world reveals welcome opportunities for all beings. As guests in this world, we can resolve to leave it a better place. The choice is ours, for we have the skillful means we require.

Let us wake up now, opening the doors to abundance, cherishing in our hearts the treasures we discover. All of us are worthy of such fulfillment, of touching the wholeness that has been closed to us.

The light of knowledge already illuminates our minds and hearts. Aware of its presence, we can allow knowledge to expand into the whole of our lives. The results can appear almost at once. Through the magic of the mind, we can make use of awareness and concentration to open the spirit of mind: We learn from the mind and for the mind and give back what we have learned to the mind. Actively exercising knowledge, we create more knowledge, sharing this abundance freely. As we learn to open doors for others as well as for ourselves, our work can have a lasting influence.

Exercise 70   Light of Knowledge

Imagine that one day you and a few others wake up to the potential for knowledge. Perhaps there are eight of you, perhaps ten, perhaps twenty-five. Suddenly all obstacles to knowledge dissolve, and you know directly how to operate awareness, concentration, and energy to generate satisfaction and enjoyment in whatever you do. Free to create great beauty and joy through working effectively, you open also to the joys of contemplation. As you manifest this precious knowledge, your actions shine brightly in the world. You offer this light to bring harmony to your own life and to the world, as you might offer a candle in a ceremony of transformation.

Suppose that the light of each candle offered in this way inspires ten more people to wake up, and each of them in turn inspires ten more. In a short time thousands upon thousands of candles are burning brightly, each reflecting light to every other candle. A whole universe of light blazes forth, an offering to clear up the darkness that clouds the human heart.

As a ritual of celebration for such potential, you may wish to enact this vision of knowledge illuminating being everywhere. Every night for a week or a month, you could light a candle to honor the light of knowledge within your mind and heart and to light the way for others. Imagine your candle, rich with the highest knowledge, transmitting its light to ten more candles, and each of these ten lighting ten more. Continue until the darkness of night for as far as you can see is illuminated by beautiful light.

Working
for the World

We have come to a point in world history that demands from us a real change. The current transformations in global society threaten the traditions of knowledge on which people have relied for millennia, and the knowledge offered in their place is limited in scope and application. Yet these same changes also present a special opportunity: to bring the light of knowledge into the very heart of the ordinary world through the daily activity of working and earning our livelihood. Facing this challenge is the work that we have been chosen to do.

The alterations sweeping through the world today are having their impact on the way we work, as they are in every other area of human endeavor. As technology becomes increasingly sophisticated, the majority of the population is being directed into labor that has no intrinsic challenge or reward. Those at the top of the social structure face a different challenge: Trained to focus their creative energies ever more narrowly on technological advances and solutions, they are learning to attune their thinking to the logic of machines and are forgetting the inner

224

meaning of work. At every level of society, the work ethic that served previous generations is losing its underlying power and conviction.

These developments put our whole modern way of life at risk. The democratic ideal insists that each individual must take responsibility for his or her own life and for the welfare of society as well. If industrial society continues to undermine the possibilities for meaningful work, this ideal will eventually fail, and people everywhere will become increasingly disoriented and unstable. Caught up in fantasies, incapable of discipline, they will express their frustration in violence and the search for superficial satisfactions. Society will reap the harvest in a dynamic of disease, disorder, and decline.

Although we can see these tendencies in operation already, what is going on in society today may offer just a small foretaste of what the future could bring. If work in the traditional sense becomes obsolete, the consequences could exceed our worst imaginings. Today we struggle to balance the budget and restore order to the environment, but these enormous problems shrink to insignificance when compared to the possibility that the whole basis for meaning in our lives could be near collapse.

In turning to work as a source of knowledge, we challenge this destructive trend. Work teaches the value of caring about what we do with our time and the significance of taking responsibility for our actions. It offers us the clarity of awareness, the nourishment of concentration, and the enjoyment of energy. Knowing how to value the quality of work, how to use it to become more concentrated, energetic, and disciplined, how to develop innovative and creative ideas and put them into practice: These are the keys to a meaningful life and to making a worthwhile contribution to the world. The knowledge we refine and perfect in this way can generate the sensitivity and vision that restore balance and sanity to the world.

Having seen its value, we have a responsibility to bring this way of working into being and pass it on to others. If we fail to do so, if we lack the inner discipline and conviction to cultivate our abilities and positive energies, we risk harm that reaches far beyond what happens in our own lives and businesses. The shortages we perpetuate today will contribute to social bankruptcy tomorrow. When the future reveals the consequences of our present actions and decisions, the chance to go in a different direction will already be gone. The time for choosing knowledge and awareness is now.

Benefactors in Life

Work has always been linked to the idea of production: making a contribution and bringing something of value into the world. Today that notion takes on added levels of significance. At this critical juncture, when so much is at stake, we need to be providers, not takers—masters of work and life rather than products of the prevailing trends.

Each of us can be a pioneer leading others to better ways of working and living. Our work, whatever form it takes, can be a splendid gesture of creation. Through making a commitment to work as a path of knowledge and transformation, we can help assure that knowledge continues to be available through the turns and tumbles of the unpredictable times to come. Long after the specific products we bring into being have vanished, the ways of working and living that we have preserved for humanity can help to make the world a worthwhile place to be.

When our vision of work and action embraces shortages and obstacles of all kinds as challenges to be transformed, we become benefactors in life. As we learn how to operate knowledge in more fruitful ways, the benefits of skillful means manifest with ever greater power and clarity, and we are showered with ever increasing benedictions. We can pass these benefits on to others, creating a positive momentum that is sorely needed in these troubled times. We can keep alive the joy that comes from living with purpose and vision.

In fulfilling our responsibility to society we also fulfill our responsibility to ourselves. When we are blessed with unshakable motivation and a confidence born of knowledge, we respond to each new situation swiftly and with power. Filled with appreciation for all that life has to offer, we find our interest flowing naturally toward activities that uplift and benefit others. The momentum that our acts engender drives out all dissatisfaction; it evokes a whole new personality. At last we can enact the vision that has long sustained our secret aspirations.

As knowledge and achievement come into balance through our work, our lives embrace the rhythms of fulfillment. We see the effects in our own experience, in our body and mind, in our sheltering environment, and in a broadening circle that embraces the whole of society. Aware of our thoughts, our senses, our actions, and their consequences, aware of being aware, we find that work becomes a gateway to realization.

Tomorrow is closer to the future than today. It is important to act now, to make use of the understanding we have at this moment instead of allowing it to fade. Work can be the body of our accomplishment, with awareness its backbone and concentration its two strong legs. With the energy of the mind coursing through our being, we awaken to knowledge and find that we have the power to make important contributions to the world.

Reflections
for My Students

Working for the Dharma gives us the opportunity to offer the West new forms of knowledge that benefit others as well as ourselves. Twenty-five years ago, knowledge of the traditional Dharma elements—the symbols, the artistic heritage, the texts—was scarcely available in the West. Almost no one knew how to build a stupa, and few people had training in Buddhist art or detailed understanding of the Tibetan Buddhist canon. Today we know much more about these things, and we are steadily learning how to transplant Eastern ways of understanding into this society. At the same time we have been able to develop valuable new skills that stimulate our creativity on a daily basis.

Bringing the traditional Dharma elements to the West is one aspect of transmitting the Dharma, but the teachings of the Buddha go beyond these outer forms to inner understanding that transforms the heart and mind. Learning to embody this understanding and manifest it in ways that suit the modern world is the deeper aspect of our guiding vision.

The method we have chosen to bring the teachings alive is through our way of working. By making our work a training in awareness, concentration, and energy, we test our understanding, our commitment, and our willingness to take responsibility. These qualities have always been necessary for spiritual development; what we are doing is putting them at the center of our practice in a new way. This is the level at which we aim to practice skillful means.

Many of the spiritual organizations that began in the 1960s with a sense of innocence and idealism have had difficulty maturing and surviving as times have changed, but our focus on skillful means has allowed us to deal with each new transition in turn. Because we value the work we do and do not separate it from our practice and our ideals, we have been successful in dealing with practical needs. By focusing on work as a practice, we have been able to make ourselves self-sufficient as a community, maximize what we can accomplish with our limited resources, and make some modest contributions that I am sure will have lasting benefit. From this perspective, skillful means makes common sense: It is the approach we have had to develop in order to accomplish our goals.

But the skillful means approach is more than this: It is an experiment in how to express and communicate the Dharma. The modern world values results, and skillful means is a way that works. By working with skillful means, we demonstrate the teachings in action. Our work becomes a gesture of good will toward society, for if we can succeed in embodying the Dharma in our work, we can pass on this vit understanding.

Practicing through Work

It is not easy to explain to others exactly what we are doing and why. Those who follow a more traditional spiritual approach often wonder why we spend so much time working, and even ask what the difference is between working in our community and working in a regular business or factory. Those who are concerned with material success may appreciate our accomplishments, but do not understand their underlying significance. They may wonder why we do not put our effort into something that has immediate practical benefit for society.

Our answer to both these questions must come through our work. If we can truly make our work into our practice, others interested in spiritual growth will eventually see that this way of practicing the Dharma has benefit. If our work has long-term benefits for ourselves and for others, then those who judge by results will see that our efforts have value. Others have chosen different approaches, but my own view is that for us this way of communicating the teachings is more effective than inspiring ceremonies and discourses.

I am satisfied with our work on a practical level, for we have been able to make small but significant contributions to preserving and transmitting the Dharma teachings. Our efforts to help Tibetan refugees, support the World Peace Ceremony, preserve and distribute Tibetan texts and art, and establish a home for the Dharma in the West have all borne fruit. Volume Four of the *Annals of the Nyingma Lineage in America*, which is being published at the same time as this book, serves as a good reminder of what we have been able to accomplish.

Compassion and Caring

Still, the question remains: Have we been able to put the Dharma into practice through our way of working? Have we been able to develop awareness, concentration, and energy and apply them in our lives? And even if the answer is yes, does this mean we are actually embodying the teachings of the Buddha?

In Mahayana Buddhism, there is a strong emphasis on uniting wisdom and compassion. Perhaps the relation between awareness and wisdom seems fairly clear, but how is awareness related to compassion? This may be the crucial point.

The connection we are looking for comes through caring. In order to see clearly what is happening in our lives, we must be willing to look. Often, however, we refuse to look, because we are afraid of what we will discover. If we see something painful or difficult, we will have to act on it, and if we act, we may fail or may provoke unwanted reactions.

To avoid this outcome, we may simply choose not to look in the first place, or else decide not to act on what we see. But the only way to support this deliberate ignoring is by not allowing ourselves to care. Without caring, we cannot develop compassion: not for the suffering of others; not even for our own suffering. Instead, we have to commit ourselves to supporting the status quo. No matter what theories we maintain, our actions proclaim that things in samsara are all right.

The skillful means approach counteracts this pattern of ignoring and forgetting. It starts with the recognition that none of this would have to happen if we had confidence in our ability to act. It is because our guts are weak that our heart is closed, and it is because our heart is closed that our throat tightens and will not let us feel what is really happening.

If we focus on work and commit ourselves to succeeding in what we do, this focused concentration strengthens the gut and frees our energy to move through the body. Knowing we can get good results, we can let our heart open. We no longer need to be afraid to experience our own caring.

Based on caring, we can commit ourselves to being honest about what we are doing with our lives and accomplishing with our time. Our honesty promotes awareness, and awareness stimulates the power of our intelligence and our five senses. Newly alive to experience, the throat opens, so that understanding flows into the heart, completing the circle.

With our head, our heart, and our guts united, we can accomplish something meaningful for ourselves and beneficial for others, and enjoy a steady stream of understanding and insight. This is a skillful means way of uniting wisdom and compassion: the Dharma in action for the modern world.

A Universal Path

Working with skillful means, we can follow a spiritual path no matter what our role in society or what particular job we have. We can practice the teachings of the Buddha without turning away from our ordinary responsibilities, and we can establish a path that others can follow as well.

When we give our energy fully to this goal, we can let its beauty inspire the heart. Looking with new honesty at our lives and at the needs of others, we can take full responsibility. Almost without realizing it, we become well-established on the spiritual path.

This same approach is equally available for others. Many people today know that they are wasting their time at work and have even learned to consider this normal. Working for the money they can make, they learn to take a very limited view of their own capabilities. Their energy and creativity go into wishful thinking and the pursuit of pleasure. How wonderful if through our actions we could demonstrate a better way!

Work can be difficult, but the real difficulty comes when people do not see that work can also be a rich source of satisfaction and enjoyment. In our own community we have had to struggle with this insight, because the people who tend to be drawn to Buddhism in this society do not necessarily have a strong work orientation. But little by little we have made progress. We have learned to cooperate despite our differences and to stick to our commitments; we have learned that the real test of our understanding is action and the real test of compassion is what we do for others without undue concern for our own impulses and desires. Because people have had good consciousness and right willingness, something positive has come about.

I think that in the past twenty-five years we have succeeded in demonstrating that people on a spiritual path do know something about work. Without any special training, we have learned to be successful at construction, metalwork, writing and publishing, book production, printing, sales, teaching, art projects, gardening and landscaping, meditation, and much more. In the future we can open our horizons to philosophy, service work, and professional skills of different kinds; we can practice Buddhist prayers and ceremonies and cultivate traditional visualizations, the reciting of sacred texts, and more formal meditation.

Even though we still have much to learn, I think we already have something of value to share with others. The more we challenge ourselves in our work, the more we will enjoy what we do and the more we will have to offer.

Through our deepening understanding, we can generate the power and motivation to become a truly positive influence on others. But for this to happen, we must first learn to manifest these teachings in our lives. This is a real path of compassion, and an opportunity to share the benefits we have received from the Dharma.

In practicing skillful means from a Dharma perspective, our tools are awareness, concentration, and energy. In this we are no different from anyone else. If we expect to do more than others, the basis will be solid commitment, genuine caring, and steady practice. If we make it our goal to let our experience and our action manifest our best understanding, the results will be worthwhile.

Path of Sharing

Approached with an attitude of enjoyment and celebration, our work is an ongoing occasion for growth, a continuing challenge, a meditation that is ultimately inseparable from samadhi. Once we understand this for ourselves, we can challenge experience with enjoyment and share our knowledge with our co-workers and friends. I recommend that we do this. The more we share, the more we will learn. We can only benefit by sharing with others.

Responding to the demands of our work, we can refine what we have learned and pass it on through our example. We can make good decisions, delegate clearly, encourage responsibility, and support leadership in others. We can follow up in a dependable way, be accountable ourselves, and ask others to be accountable as well. We can create positive feelings, thoughts, and gestures that uplift and inspire the quality of our work. We can do our part to keep the environment we work in clean and beautiful.

Beyond this, we can encourage and support others through a light, humorous attitude that expresses caring and affection and warms people's hearts. We can offer suggestions to help others be more aware, more concentrated and energetic. We can share the key insights that have helped us to wake up; we can share the small steps that have made an essential difference in our lives. We can make charts and diagrams to show how we have connected key insights and steps of development, organizing this knowledge so it is easy for others to learn and understand. We can encourage co-workers to try new things and develop in new ways, and we can ask for and encourage the best in everyone. We can cultivate the wish that others might learn more quickly than we have learned, and do whatever we can to make that wish come true.

As we learn appreciation for the guiding vision of the Dharma and for how its patterns manifest in each project we undertake, we can be grateful for what each of our colleagues is contributing to the success of our efforts. We can respect the strengths of our co-workers and sincerely wish them well in transforming their weaknesses into strengths. We can resolve to take advantage of this opportunity to work, to learn, and to share our understanding with others, cultivating the honesty, integrity, and discipline to put our resolve into practice. We can enjoy the interplay of knowledge and time with awareness, concentration, and energy.

Gestures of Giving

Within our community we have the opportunity to express kindness, cooperate with one another, and build respect. Such practice leads to greater understanding, helping us to create good friendships and a balanced way of life within which we can develop and grow. Although there may be higher levels of accomplishment, success at this level can do much to make experience satisfactory and enjoyable, and open the path to realization and fulfillment.

Each society has its own modes of expression and its own subtle nuances of communication. I especially appreciate the friendly accommodating politeness that is taught in this society, for while my understanding is fairly good, I am not always successful in communicating well at this level. Everyone from diplomats to store salespeople knows that speaking kindly to one another has a positive effect, even if we are not wholly sincere. At the level of our ordinary consciousness, kind words and small acts of recognition set off ripples of positive energy that inspire us and make us happier.

Cultivating kindness, friendship, giving, and helpful ways of being from day to day, we can create a positive alternative to the destructive attitudes that bring such great suffering to individuals and even to whole cultures. As we step into positions where we can influence others or exercise power and control, we should learn not to rely on force and negativity to achieve our aims, but to put our own ideals into practice—not just today or tomorrow, but from this moment forward.

Standing in the lineage of a great spiritual tradition, we have much to pass on, for many great masters have made us remarkable gifts of knowledge. Their compassionate generosity has led them to give the greatest gift of all: knowledge of how to develop human consciousness. Always remember that this gift is meant to be shared. If we take the knowledge we have discovered in this lifetime with us when we die, our life does not have much worth.

Sharing what we learn is our gesture of giving. Our contribution may not be great, but if we have glimpsed a higher knowledge, we can find ways to transmit it, uplifting the quality of life for the sake of future generations. As we carry out our everyday responsibilities, we can manifest patience, endurance, and compassion. If we all give what we can, there will be good results and continuing benefits.

APPENDIX

Tools for Transformation

Tools for Change

Exercise A   Silence, Clarity, and Ease

This exercise relaxes the body and refreshes the flow of mental activity, and is especially helpful when you feel confused or dull. It creates a cushion of rejuvenating awareness, concentration, and energy that sharpens focus and concentration and stabilizes your efforts, supporting you in whatever you do.

The exercise can be practiced whenever you wish. There are three parts, linked to breath, body, and mind. To become familiar with the exercise, practice three times a day, focusing on the body in the morning and evening and on the breath in the afternoon. As the exercise becomes more familiar, the shift to mental activity will develop naturally. Later you can also practice the aspect related to mind separately, twice a day or more.

Posture is important in this exercise. Sit on a cushion or in a chair so the backbone is straight but not stiff. Rest the hands on the knees, and tuck the chin in slightly so there is a small curve at the Adam's apple and the spine at the back of the neck straightens a little. Gently loosen and relax the shoulders, so the line of the neck and shoulder forms a natural downward curve. Let the mouth be slightly open, with the teeth very slightly parted. Relax the muscles of the upper jaw a little, as if just beginning to smile. Notice any tension in or behind the eyes and see if you can relax it. The eyes can be half open, without looking at anything in particular.

Breath

Lightly pay attention to the breath, breathing through both nose and mouth. This way of breathing is unusual and may be uncomfortable at first, but it has an energizing effect, and soon you will find it easier and more pleasant to continue.

Once you are comfortable with this way of breathing, sense the flow of the breath as it moves out of the body and then returns. You could imagine that the breath goes out horizontally like a river flowing slowly across a plain, and then comes back. Alternately, the flow of the outbreath may form a gentle curve downward that becomes a ring or circle completed by the inbreath. In either case, gently focus on the flowing movement of the breath along the whole length of its path. Touching the breath with awareness, you may find that you can follow the flow out ten inches or so. Without straining, be especially sensitive to the beginning and end of each breath.

At first there will be a little tension in the going in and out. As breathing continues, this tension will subside, and the movement will simply go on by itself—there is no need to direct it. As the body settles, the breath naturally becomes calmer and lighter.

Body

As you feel the breath flowing in and out of the body, you may gradually become aware of a soft feeling of warmth in the neck and throat. Appreciate and enjoy this soft warmth, merging it with the awareness that follows it, and let it become richer and deeper. Gradually let the warmth spread down to the shoulders and heart and up to the head, and from there to the whole body, deep into the tissues, muscles, and organs, and even into the cells.

This same gentle warmth can also pass into the space immediately surrounding the body. Imagine that this space itself becomes warm, soft, gentle, calm, and quiet. The quality of this space is soothing and happy, relaxing to the body deep within.

Touching this quiet silence with awareness, you may sense its soft warmth expanding several inches beyond the skin. See if you can sensitively explore the warmth, playing with its edges. It may expand more and more, until it is double the size of the body. Inside, the body is calm; outside all is soft and quiet. Gently the senses can appreciate these feelings, merging inside and outside into silent, quiet space.

The fuller the silence, the deeper the relaxation. As mental instructions lessen, the body becomes more settled and space opens up, allowing energy to flow freely both inside and outside the body. This interaction between inner and outer is like swimming in a still pool at nightfall, calm and joyful. Throat, head, belly, and heart are loose; the silence is like a baby sleeping.

Mind

Whatever tension remains is due to the activity of mind. Now, however, the stillness and silence of the breath and body slow down and relax all of the senses, including mind. Vivid images, memories, and insights may come to mind, but you can let them go. Instructions and dialogues become fewer, until words like 'letting go' or 'trying' no longer apply. At this point, no vehicle is needed; an inner instructor or watcher is not helpful.

With deepening silence, the mind's awareness loosens and relaxes into accommodation. Awareness contacts thought directly, without images. The chain of thoughts, one leading to another, becomes less tense; the speed of self-created thought slows. Gradually, motion and momentum cease, leading toward the complete silence of contemplation. There is no relationship in which to hold an image; silence itself is the image. There is no past, present, or future, no parent of experience—just being completely alone, silent. The more still we are, the more we can almost taste and hear the silence. Within this silence, we are completely awake.

Inner Transformation

By practicing this exercise, you can discover ease wherever you are and whatever you are doing. In the middle of sound there is silence; in the midst of momentum the energy is silent and still.

Such silence brings essential relaxation that rejuvenates both energy and awareness. Energy can take hold of time, recharging itself and restoring an open flow that dissolves emotional imbalances and vitalizes thought. A sense of full openness makes a new spirit available. It is like becoming a new person.

This exercise comes easily to the presence of those who practice it. Simply remembering the experience of the exercise will help you to relax while you work. When the experience is more familiar, recalling it will activate the feeling of ease.

Although there are higher levels of contemplation and meditation, this first level of relaxation is all you need to work skillfully. Additional instructions relating to further practice will vary according to the kind of work being done, the purposes to which awareness, concentration, and energy are being directed, and the temperament of the individual.

Exercise B Working Relaxation

You can develop relaxation as you work by bringing awareness to body sensations and cultivating a quality of light concentration. Be lightly aware of each feeling or sensation. Perhaps you feel a tightness in the throat, pressure at the temples, or constriction in the belly. Awareness helps these feelings of tightness to dissolve. As you learn to relax and open the senses, body and mind become integrated and balanced, and experience becomes richer, healthier, and more beautiful.

Exercise C   Opening Throat Energy

Relax tension throughout the body and let the body grow very calm. Let go of any worrying or negative imaginations and let the mind rest in silence as much as possible. Now invite a soft warm breath into the throat. Let it spread to the back of the neck, and to the head at eye level. Gradually let this warm energy flow in a ring through and around the head and throat, loosening blockages. Imagine that you are massaging the warmth from within, until the head and throat feel as though they are floating in feeling. As body and mind come alive together, let the warm, sensitive feeling flow into the heart as well.

Do this practice morning and evening and also throughout the day whenever problems arise and negative emotions begin to stir. You may find that better thoughts come forth, ideas become clearer, and communication improves. Nervous tension gives way to a calm and sharp presence that is both pleasant and highly energized.

Exercise D   Visualizing Positive Energy

In the morning, right after waking up, do some simple stretches to loosen the body. Then sit quietly with the back straight and breathe deeply, exhaling fully three times through both nose and mouth. Let body and mind become completely silent. This silence can be so deep and full there are no thoughts.

248

From within silence, let positive energy and positive thoughts arise. Visualize the actions you plan for the day ahead in a positive light, and imagine positive feelings radiating throughout the entire day to come and beyond to the full expanse of your life. Remind yourself that you are preparing not just for a single day, but for the whole future. Wish from your heart for a beautiful life, and let good thoughts and feelings flow freely. Continue for five or ten minutes.

Exercise E Appreciating Accomplishment

In the evening before going to bed, do a few simple stretches, then sit with the back straight, breathe deeply, and exhale fully three times through both nose and mouth. Looking back on what you did during the day, appreciate and enjoy each step of accomplishment, each positive thought and action. Where you could have done better, resolve to improve. Embrace all of your actions with positive energy, and let this energy stay with you as you go to sleep.

Exercise F Gestures of Sensitivity

A. *Positive Posture* Whenever you feel the pressure of emotions, take an expansive posture: Smile broadly, let the eyes open wide and light up, relax the throat, throw the shoulders back and open up the chest. By coordinating awareness with the body, this posture promotes energy flow and stimulates fresh, clear energy.

B. *Time of Day* Try this practice whenever you think of it: In the morning be especially sensitive to the flow of energy in the head, in the afternoon be sensitive to the throat and heart, and in the evening be sensitive to the heart.

C. *Balance in the Throat*   To develop balance between the energy centers, monitor the throat center throughout the day, keeping it relaxed and open. The energy should be neither too soft nor too tense and threatening. Periodically check each of the other centers: How clear is the head, how open is the heart, and how steady is the gut?

Exercise G   One Small Step

Here is a short-term goal you can practice at any time. Tell yourself: "Today I will not make discouraging pronouncements to myself or to other people." If you succeed in doing this, congratulate yourself. Remember that there are many people who would be unable to take such a step, and dedicate your success to their welfare.

Exercise H   Practicing Compassion

Develop a willingness to be open-minded, helpful, and understanding. Practice toward others whatever you wish for yourself. Look carefully at points where this seems unworkable; for example, in dealing with competitors. Is there really a conflict?

Exercise I   Finding Sore Points

Think of each area of your work and responsibility. Are you facing each one fully? Where are the uncomfortable points for you personally: taking care of details, learning new skills, staying on schedule, taking care of equipment, developing teamwork? The feeling of not wanting to look is a good indicator that you should investigate that particular topic.

Exercise J Staying on Time

A. Whenever you create structures in time, it is important to challenge yourself to stay within the rhythms you have set up. For a week, try structuring your time tightly in order to meet specific goals, and observe yourself carefully and precisely. When do you maintain this discipline? When do you fail to do so? How can you improve your ability to stay 'on target'? Does keeping to this structure make you feel pressured? If so, can you trace the mental patterns that produce this reaction?

B. Set up a weekly calendar and assign different tasks and projects to specific time slots. Group tasks together in ways that preserve the rhythms appropriate to each type of work. Observe yourself over several weeks. How successfully can you maintain this structure? Do not be concerned with your failures, but allow feedback from your positive results to encourage further efforts.

Exercise K Combining Tasks

Try putting different small tasks together into a corner of time, so that you can get them all done in a row. Learn to think in terms of multiple goals: Can a report, a material, or a trip be used for two different purposes, saving time and energy?

Exercise L Completing Tasks

Make it a discipline not to leave bits and pieces of unfinished work behind you, so that the mind stays unencumbered, ready for careful thought and action.

A. 'Just Do It'. See Exercise 8, p. 37.

B. Try setting aside half an hour a day to do small tasks; resolve to get as much as possible done in that time. Make sure to stop when the half hour is up. What results do you observe?

C. If a task does remain incomplete, practice leaving it in good order so that it is easy to return to it.

Exercise M Letting Go

Some people have trouble letting go of a task or project: They constantly return to it, trying to improve on the finished product. If this is an issue for you, you can make it a practice to break this pattern. For instance, when something is finished, let it stay finished. What results do you observe?

Tools for
Troubled Times

In any kind of work or business we may encounter intensely frustrating times when all our resources seem to be in short supply: Our crew is too small; staff members are emotional and dissatisfied and their energy level is weak; funding has run out; the project is behind schedule; we lack the proper materials or tools; unexpected emergencies arise.

At such times we may experience great agitation. As conflict builds in body and mind, we feel panicky, grow obsessive about making mistakes, or explode into anger, blaming ourselves or others for our difficulties. Unable to be open with others, we may make enemies without knowing how it happened. Our intelligence seems to shut down: Our view contracts into self-pity or paranoia or rage, and we feel incompetent and neurotic or hopeless and victimized. Caught up in negative thoughts and images, we almost seem to encourage the negativity. Our energy becomes tight and restricted, emotions take over, and we lose control over our lives. Whole days can pass in a blur.

These are the times to redouble our efforts to free ourselves from emotionality and be more fully aware. The following exercises may help in these efforts. They focus primarily on generating gut-level energy to relieve negativity, open the heart, and stimulate the flow of energy through all the body centers. Exercise P also relieves emotionality and promotes a light awareness.

Exercise N   Building Self-Healing Gut Energy

A. Sit quietly and relax tensions in the body. Concentrating on the belly, exhale fully, relaxing the abdomen. Then inhale and hold the breath in the gut, holding the abdomen in a little. Still holding the breath, energize the gut, creating warmth there. Make the belly area bigger, relaxing into the feeling that arises. Feel the energy; let your body be sensitive and relaxed, smooth and light like milk mixed with water. Hold to the point of discomfort or a little longer, then very slowly release and sit quietly for a few minutes before repeating. Do the exercise three or nine times in all.

After each repetition, while you are sitting quietly, let inner warmth rising from the belly calm and relax the field of contemplation. Distribute this feeling throughout the body: into the cells, tissues, organs, and muscles; inside the tissues of the face and neck, the back, chest and arms, the hands and fingers, legs and feet. Even thoughts and images can be bathed in warm, gentle, calm, and relaxing feelings. Let this inner massage of feeling circulate throughout the body, being sensitive to the flowing movement of warmth and energy. During the day remember the warmth of that feeling and the joy that accompanies it.

B. To extend this exercise further, concentrate lightly on the heart, and let the feeling of inner warmth generated from the belly relax and heal the heart with love and joy. Let go of any feelings of failure or guilt. Encourage awareness and give space to the full-bodied energy of cherishing what is positive. Allow yourself to appreciate your natural intelligence and caring, your strengths and abilities, and the value of the work you are doing.

C. If necessary, repeat parts A and B of this exercise every morning and evening for twenty minutes or more. After three weeks, if you are still troubled with negativity, start each session with a few minutes of head rotations, leg stretches, belly circles (see Exercise 26, *Kum Nye Relaxation*, Part 1), and side stretches (see Exercise 21, *Kum Nye Relaxation*, Part 1); then sit quietly for about five minutes, enjoying the feelings and sensations, before doing the practice given here.

Exercise O   Opening the Energy of the Gut

Whenever you discover escapism, excuses, and procrastination coming to the foreground as you work, switch your focus from words and images in the head to the energy of the gut. If you have difficulty making this shift, remind yourself of the goals for which you are working, and let these 'reasons' turn into feelings in the heart. Relax the belly and connect the belly with the feelings in the heart.

Exercise P Halo of Luminous Warmth

During the day, you can support positive thoughts and images by letting a luminous quality come into the head. When you have the chance, sit quietly with eyes closed and visualize light entering the top of the forehead and then arcing outward and down, to the left and right, back and front, forming a halo that surrounds the whole body. Let yourself float within this warm, luminous field.

This field of warmth and light can become like space, surrounding the body. It can also expand into the body, occupying each cell. The feeling tone is one of being free from tension, completely released from entanglements. The quality of life seems light, easy, open, with a full, rich flavor that is very comfortable and inviting. Bring this quality into your daily work. To extend and deepen the practice, go to sleep at night within the halo of light.

Exercise Q Connecting Head and Belly

When difficulties arise during the day, the awareness of the head needs the support of strong, concentrated gut-energy. To marry these two centers, open the throat wide, relax the lower neck, and let your breath flow softly and gently. Relax the belly and breathe softly but deeply into the gut. Continue for a minute or so before returning to work.

Good
Business Practices

The suggestions given here may be useful to people who are inexperienced in business and to newly-formed non-profit organizations with volunteer staff. We have learned their value through experience, and hope they can help others avoid costly mistakes or wasted time and effort.

Records and Manuals A clear and disciplined attitude is expressed in maintaining good records and files, especially financial records, and in clear written descriptions of the procedures and jobs associated with each department or function in your business or project. Checklists and manuals on how to perform various tasks and operate and maintain machines support sharing and help to keep the quality of work high. If such tasks are allowed to slip, the people responsible can be reminded without blame and without supporting excuses.

Knowing Exact Profits As every businessperson well knows, knowing the exact profit margin of a project or enterprise gives a precise picture of what is happening. If the bottom line is weak, it is time to reflect on basics. For instance, considering the competition, what does your business have to offer: quality, service, fast timing, specialized knowledge? How can profits be increased?

Guarding Resources By guarding your resources and staying on top of the unexpected, you protect your ability to reach your goals. Good business decisions will not put any of the organization's resources at undue risk—money, vehicles, tools, or materials. Money spent without advance planning for some exceptional purpose should be responsibly reported without delay.

Exploring Alternatives Exploring alternatives can cut costs, increase options, and open whole new possibilities. Alternatives can include alternate vendors, new estimates, different materials, different schedules, and different ways to organize the work. Take the time to create several projections for each job; at the same time be sure that this kind of research does not become an excuse for inaction.

Dealing with Money Small expenditures, say under $20, are often ignored or taken for granted, but over time they can add up to thousands of dollars. If your project wastes just $5 a day, this is over $1000 a year. To cultivate appreciation for money as a resource, try paying special attention to your own personal expenses. When you make a small purchase, watch for careless thoughts such as "This doesn't matter," "Oh, why not?" "I'll never notice the difference." What happens if you bring more careful consideration to even the smallest expense?

Legal Ramifications Learning about legal requirements ahead of time helps to avoid costly mistakes. People tend to feel uncomfortable with legal questions, and this makes legal issues a prime candidate for misunderstanding, lack of communication, insufficient caution, or not enough attention to detail. Clear and timely communication on potential legal concerns to the appropriate person within the organization or to legal advisers is vital for protecting the organization from possible harm.

Checking Safety and Quality Special work teams or task forces formed to oversee quality control, safety, productivity, and organizational structures can cut through structures that tend to become rigid over time. A clear path of decision and a path of action will allow the task-force knowledge to be enacted.

Creating Financial Reserves Every business needs a safety margin to protect against difficulties, mistakes, lost time, wasted efforts, bad investments, or uncontrollable circumstances. Here is a rule of thumb: A one-year-old business should have enough money in reserve to run the business for one month with no income at all; a two-year-old business should have two months of reserves, and so forth.

Sharing Knowledge Managers can work with each task force or project crew to determine what information should be freely available. For example, letting each person in a project know the costs of the project stimulates a higher level of responsibility in everyone. What are the costs of each project in time, energy, manpower, money, and inventory? Exactly how much does it cost to open the doors each day for business, including the operating expenses? As each hour passes, how much money is being spent? What are the costs of typical materials? What are the underlying debts and liabilities with which the business must contend?

If you yourself do not have this kind of information, you can ask for it. Be prepared to demonstrate why it is valuable for this kind of information to be shared. How much is being spent each day on the work that you do? How much money is actually wasted when a mistake is made? For different projects interesting ratios can be calculated that give each person a vivid sense of the value of the materials and services being used.

Widely shared knowledge of schedules also supports good teamwork. Each project coordinator can create and share monthly, weekly, and daily schedules with all members of the team. If you do not have such schedules, ask for them as a way of developing a broader sense of responsibility.

Knowing the Qualities Required As an organization takes shape, the leadership needs to know the qualities required by each position and the individual handling that position needs to know what he or she is striving toward. Descriptions of the qualities needed can be made for each job. Note that the emphasis here is on qualities which can be developed through the work.

For example, an administrative assistant or executive secretary needs very particular qualities:

clarity and sharpness; the ability to keep things in mind and not forget details; the ability to remind oneself and others in a timely way; sensitivity that judges people accurately; communication skills and control over the voice; ability to feedback accurate information; keen awareness of the whole situation; loyalty to the organization; and the ability to keep confidentiality.

A financial officer needs to know when to spend and when not to spend; be able to question decisions made by others and check one point of view against another; operate a tight budget in the face of constant demands for more money; be careful not to risk money unless the probability of success is very high and the return on the investment is worthwhile; understand numbers and psychology and their inter-action; and understand timing, such as turnover times, the timing of purchases, and the relation of inventory to the flow of money.

Ten Questions for Reflection

What is a good cause?
What is profit?
What is the real profit?
What is investment?
What is value?
What is worthwhile?
What is long-lasting?
What is business?
What is the virtue in business?
How can the benefits be dedicated?

Index

Books by Tarthang Tulku

Gesture of Balance

Hidden Mind of Freedom

Knowledge of Freedom

Knowledge of Time and Space

Kum Nye Relaxation

Love of Knowledge

Openness Mind

Skillful Means

Skillful Means: Wake Up!

Time, Space, and Knowledge

Visions of Knowledge